HUNGARIAN
FOLK CUSTOMS

CORVINA PRESS

HUNGARIAN FOLK ART 6

Editor

Prof. GYULA ORTUTAY
Member of the Hungarian Academy of Sciences

Hungarian Folk Customs

by **TEKLA DÖMÖTÖR**

Original title: MAGYAR NÉPSZOKÁSOK
Corvina, Budapest, 1972

Translated by JUDITH ELLIOTT

Photographs by PÉTER KORNISS

Drawings by MAGDA SCHÖBERL

Map by MARIANNA KISS

© Corvina, Budapest, 1972
ISBN 963 13 0164 8

Second, revised edition

Printed in Hungary, 1977
Kossuth Printing House, Budapest
CO1478-h-7781

THE DEVELOPMENT OF HUNGARIAN FOLK CUSTOMS AND THEIR MAIN CHARACTERISTICS

Since the beginning of the nineteenth century masterly studies on Hungarian popular traditions have appeared in various journals, like, for instance, *Tudományos Gyűjtemény* [Scientific Selection] and *Felsőmagyarországi Minerva* [Upper Hungarian Minerva]. The first anthology was published in 1867 under the title of *Magyarországi népszokások* [Folk Customs in Hungary]. Sándor Réső Ensel, who compiled and assisted in the collection of data for the book, made the following observations in his introduction:

"It has long been the intention of members of literary circles in Hungary to make a collection of folk customs. In the year 1862 the Kisfaludy Society called attention to this fact in a number of newspapers; page 319 of *Vasárnapi Újság* [Sunday News] for example, contains a report justifying the value of such a collection. But the compilation of folk customs, a volume that should have appeared many years ago has still not been published to this day...

"I have travelled through most of my lovely native land and, while doing so, have always directed my attention to certain factors. I decided to acquaint myself thoroughly with the ordinary people, to study their language, dress, songs, dances, their sayings and customs. I followed them into the meadows, took part in their wedding feasts and funeral ceremonies, and all that I saw and heard was noted down in my diary with complete objectivity... By studying this collection a great deal can be learnt about the development of the ceremonies connected with marriage. We can discover how dependent the young people were on their parents, how patriarchal life was in the nation as a whole, and how great a father's power was over his children. We can also learn about the tradition of having witnesses and a best man, about the development of the actual marriage ceremony, and about the long period of bargaining and argument before agreement was reached for a girl to be given away in marriage. The information will acquaint us with the period of courtship, the wedding breakfast and the interesting tradition in which the cooks collected money from the guests with their hands bandaged. Scenes of gay dancing and music, with crowds of young people and an atmosphere of boisterous jocularity, the passing round of the wine and the ceremonial processions appear before our eyes. Many jovial speeches and poems are delivered during the proposal, the farewell party to the bride and the marriage ceremony...

"Since 1848 great changes have occurred. If one compares the customs practised before the revolution with those that have become popular since, great differences can be found, indicated in all sections of the populace from two periods that follow one another closely... These great changes in traditional customs were induced by the circumstances connected with the 1848 revolution, which brought an end to the former conditions of feudal serfdom. Folk customs were affected by this severe upheaval, by the political changes that shook the nation to its very roots, by the suspension of the constitution, the introduction of various direct and indirect taxes and other adverse circumstances...

"Many good, useful and beautiful traits are implied in these rich national customs... Most of the bad customs, that would hinder our spiritual and moral development, and are regarded as destructive vermin in popular life anyway, have been omitted..."

It is by no means unintentional that we have quoted Sándor Késő Ensel at such length. For the quotation shows the manifold nature of folk customs. The role of socio-economic and aesthetic elements are of equal importance as components in creating a pattern of life, in which the traditional culture of the village has developed. Almost a century after the above-quoted observations were made by Késő Ensel, Gyula Ortutay wrote a paper (Questionnaire on the Collection of Nativity Plays), in which he listed and analysed the manifold artistic and functional elements that must be taken into consideration when studying folk customs, namely the manifest and hidden aim of the customs, the material background, social role and the aesthetic components—the songs, dances, poetic wording and choreography.

Sándor Késő Ensel's introduction is up-to-date from another aspect, too, for he was aware that historical changes were reflected in folk customs. He is in this respect far more "modern" than quite a few of the romantic ethnographers in the first decades of this century, who looked first and foremost for the ancient and unchanged elements in folk customs. Késő Ensel was a witness of one of the great turning points in the life of the Hungarian peasantry—the abolition of serfdom—and so was able to study and write down the consequent changes that appeared in Hungarian village life.

It is worthwhile considering the question of "good and bad customs" a

I. The Nativity players. Kéty. Tolna County, 1971 ▶

little longer. Throughout the centuries it has been the ruling classes who have decided, from their own point of view, which customs were good and which were bad. The fact that it is precisely this that enables us to reconstruct the past history of our folk customs is an interesting contradiction. The more educated members of the ruling classes were not really interested in spending time studying the traditions of the ordinary people and writing them down. What we know about the past history of folk customs is mainly a result of the judgment that the church and administrative organs passed over them, referring to some as evil and forbidding their practice. In the Middle Ages the Christian Church regarded all customs that had survived from old Hungarian culture as "heathen" and therefore evil. Sixteenth-century Protestant preachers classified many Roman Catholic customs as perverse. In the past, administrative bodies have always declared those customs bad and subversive which involved large groups of people that might disturb law and order. It was for this reason that they condemned the gatherings of women for the purpose of spinning, the selection of a Whitsuntide king, the festivities on Midsummer's Day, large weddings and so on.

At the end of the eighteenth and the beginning of the nineteenth century it was the educated and enlightened individuals who regarded folk customs with suspicion and believed that they reflected nothing but backwardness and superstition, whereas the more conservative intellectuals began studying them and claimed that they contained ancient Hungarian elements.

The generation of progressive politicians, scientists and writers of the Reform Period, who prepared the way for the 1848 War of Independence, was the first to unite political interest in the ordinary people with a recognition of the aesthetic values of popular poetry and customs. They gave a new and correct interpretation to the former concept of "good or bad customs" when they recognized the progressive or retrograde nature of a certain folk custom.

The concept of folk customs

What in fact are folk customs? They are the spontaneous forms of cultural tradition, a frame within which the holidays and weekdays of the people are conducted. The members of a community voluntarily conform to the communal modes of behaviour and action that correspond to living cultural

◀ *II. The Nativity play. Kéty, Tolna County, 1971*

traditions. Folk customs are comprised of etiquette, moral codes, communal laws, art, poetry, acting, myths, and magic.

Naturally in all countries of Europe, including Hungary, written laws have controlled the communal modes of behaviour for hundreds of years in the most important aspects of life. Folk customs have survived in those spheres of peasant life where they were considered to be of such vital importance to the community that the people simply could not manage without them, or in the case of certain regions that were more or less ignored by the Church and State.

Folk customs have always determined the relationship between the different members of a community, family discipline, etiquette and the moral code of a community, and the arrangement inside a home (they determined, for example, where the various members of a family should eat and sleep).

Sometimes the higher authorities were unable to deal with popular traditions. During the period of enlightenment, for instance, a law was passed prohibiting the prodigality of village weddings, christenings and funeral ceremonies. The writer and agriculturist Sámuel Tessedik (1742–1820) reported that some of the poorer peasant families were reduced to beggary because of the lavish expenditure of the wedding. The formative force of the community, however, proved stronger than the decree, and the ceremonial festivities of the community survived in their original form.

Similar action was taken against certain rites that were considered to possess magic powers and were practised on the most important occasions in community life, at birth, death, harvest time, etc. But the people continued to carry out these practices in secret, despite all attempts to prohibit them. The reason for this action on the part of the ordinary people stemmed from a feeling of insecurity that had existed in village life.

There are customs in the village that will immediately catch the eye and others that will only be noticed after a longer stay. The festive, ceremonial customs will attract the visitor's attention immediately and, in fact, these traditions come first and foremost to mind when we think of folk customs. The traditions connected with conduct and morals, however, will only be revealed after a longer stay in the village. The superstitious, magic customs are carried out in secret, partly because people are ashamed of them and partly because secrecy is often a necessary component in the effectiveness of a magic practice.

Some customs are compulsory for all inhabitants of a village, while others are limited to a particular age group, sex or occupation. Since the fifteenth century we know, for example, of the existence of a separate carnival for women in which the presence of men was strictly forbidden. **11** Shepherds, vine growers, fishermen and so on, all had their own special ceremonial traditions.

In Sándor Réső Ensel's collection, folk customs already show great regional differences. The customs in a Catholic region, for example, differed from those in a Protestant village. In the latter, festivities were centred around the wedding, carnival, and pig killing, whereas the celebrations in Catholic Transdanubia were much more colourful and frequent. The various ethnic groups also possess their own particular customs; we know, for instance, of the ritual sequence of events at weddings in the Palots region and the special carnivals peculiar to Szatmár County.

Hungarian folk customs today are undergoing significant changes. Various factors have given rise to the gradual disappearance and complete transformation of popular traditions, namely the land reform, the structural transfiguration and technical modernization of Hungarian agriculture, the improvement of the school system, the extension of the library organization and adult education, and the nation-wide network of radio and television. The marriage between two young members of a cooperative farm is quite different from the old village weddings and new ways of celebrating name-days have also developed.

Today this book can only pass on the message from a world that is rapidly disappearing. Some customs still flourish, others can occasionally be found in isolated areas, or could be found some years ago, but many are only remembered by the older generation. Even where they have survived they are given a new interpretation, and myth and magic are transformed into poetry.

Readers will become acquainted here with the final phase in the life of Hungarian folk customs. Their development was the result of a long historical process in which the cultural traditions that the Magyar conquerors brought with them to their new home and the culture and religion that they later acquired played an important role. Hungarian folk customs were coloured by the traditions of peoples from surrounding countries and from those who lived among them. The peasantry of most East European countries lived under similar judicial, economic and cultural conditions to those in

Hungary. The collapse of feudalism, the abolition of serfdom and the struggle for an independent national existence took place at more or less the same period in history and under similar circumstances. If we are looking for the characteristically Hungarian elements in the folk customs of this country we must first of all examine the form and not the function. Similar traditions to those in Hungary, connected with man's life and the seasons of the year, can be found in neighbouring countries, but the artistic elements attached to the customs, namely folk poetry, songs and the taste for colour and form, are characteristically Hungarian.

The ceremonial customs in particular presented a good opportunity for the development of poetic forms. The wedding ceremony, carnival mummery and other spectacular customs were performed in a dramatic way and were thus very suitable occasions for the introduction of the popular poetry of the community. After the drudgery of weekdays, these ceremonial traditions brought relaxation and amusement, and an artistic experience that all culture should be privileged with.

Myth, magic, poetry

The poetic elements connected with folk customs are also known under the term of ritual poetry. This term includes greetings, quête songs, epic or lyric songs and plays. The feature they have in common is that they all appear within the framework of folk customs and are usually accompanied by some ritual action.

The action linked to these texts can vary. It sometimes takes the form of a play, very like "real" drama, with several characters. At other times the action is symbolic, like, for example, the lighting of a fire, the sprinkling of water, or a masked dance. At Whitsuntide girls in ceremonial dress select one of their companions as "little queen" and carry her in the air chanting "the flax must also grow tall". On another occasion a person appears disguised as an animal, then collapses on the ground, whereupon his companion brings him back to life with the accompaniment of amusing incantations. These are just a few examples of the rites linked to ritual folk poetry.

The melody of the songs that occasionally accompanied these magic practices is sometimes very old. Béla Bartók stated that the melodies connected with the ceremonial customs stand out from other folk tunes and form a separate group. They include the "regös" or wassailing song sung during the period between Christmas and the New Year, the wedding songs, laments and harvest songs. The enumeration of Bartók also refers to the fact that ceremonial folk customs can be classified into three main groups: **13** (1) seasonal festivities, (2) festivities connected with man's life, and (3) festivities connected with his work. Ritual poetry, therefore, appears in connections with all the above occasions.

These customs, obviously, do not originate from the same time, but came into existence at different periods in history. We can only guess at the meaning of the archaic, mythical elements, and magic formulas preserved in the oldest strata of tradition, but their beauty, on the other hand, can still be appreciated today.

How is it that these ancient melodies, charms and plays have survived until this century? For many hundreds of years the man who worked on the land and kept animals was helpless when faced with the powers of nature on which his existence depended. Fertility and good weather were of vital importance to life. So we can understand that at an early stage in the history of Hungary and other European countries, man tried to insure the fertility of the soil and the multiplication of man and animal by the use of superstitious rites; and with the help of magic formulas he endeavoured to avert hail, storms and other strokes of fate. These magic practices were repeated year after year within the framework of traditional folk customs.

Ritual poetry of course does not only consist of incantations. The original function of a significant section was always purely aesthetic, with the aim of rendering the ceremonies attractive and memorable occasions by adding songs, dances and plays. But the old superstitious meaning of the magical songs that are still sung today has been more or less forgotten. The wassailing custom, for example, has more or less lost its original magic aim. It is now an occasion for paying respects and courting, in which the boys still give greetings at each house, but more particularly at those houses where girl friends and acquaintances live.

Due to their complex nature a correct portrayal and classification of Hungarian customs has met with a great many difficulties. What we were able to record here is really only a model of the original custom, which is performed over and over again on suitable occasions. Often several versions exist for a particular custom in one single village. Certain customs exist in

different versions in the minds of the people who practise them. The older generation, for example, will refer to customs as they were when they were young, while the young people will only know the custom in its altered, pres-
14 ent-day form.

A better understanding of the various customs can often be reached by listening to people's explanations of them. These explanations are sometimes quite poetic, and the interpretations of one or two of the more complicated ceremonial customs are legends in themselves. The reasons given for the development of the old superstitious customs, however, are often based on pseudo-historic legends that tend to hide rather than reveal their true significance and purpose. People often connect the customs involving noisy scenes and masked parades with the struggles against the Turks; the spectacular masked carnival at Mohács, for example, performed by the "Sokác" people (a Slavonic ethnic group) is explained as a "memorial" custom, originally practised in order to frighten away the Turks.

It is for this reason that I have endeavoured when describing our folk customs to give not only my own opinion but also the opinion of those who practise them.

I have already mentioned that a correct description of the customs is facilitated by classifying them into groups. Several distinct groups can be formed, like, for example, customs associated with the calendar year, with the events in man's life or his work, with some historic event or communal law, etc. Further grouping can also be made, for life as a whole was greatly influenced by folk customs, with traditional medicine, witchcraft and fortune-telling also forming part of the system of these customs.

A detailed account of Hungarian folk customs with descriptions of regional and ethnic variations would extend into several volumes. We cannot, therefore, give more than a description of the most widely practised traditions, for folk culture as a whole was conditioned by popular tradition.

SEASONAL FESTIVITIES

A significant number of Hungarian folk customs are associated with the twelve calendar months. Specific rituals are connected with the changing seasons of the year, with summer and winter Solstice, with certain stages in agricultural work and with state and church festivites. They are sometimes confined to a single day, or form a cycle, like, for instance, the mid-winter, early spring and Whitsun cycles.

The majority of people who practise these customs are not aware of the fact that the seasonal traditions came into existence in very different periods in history. Reforms introduced in the calendar year gave rise to changes in dates of several customs. This is why the dates of certain traditions carried out at the beginning of the year in Hungary and other European countries vary between December 13th (St. Lucy's Day) and January 6th (Epiphany).

Although they were familiar with agriculture, the chief occupation of the Hungarian conquerors, when they first settled in Central Europe, was horse-breeding. For many centuries before their arrival in present-day Hungary, this Finno-Ugrian people lived among Turkish tribes in part of the Khazar Empire. Due to their similar behaviour and appearance, contemporary sources identified them with the Turkish equestrian people. The religion practised by the Hungarian tribes was shamanistic. We can assume that the ceremonial customs of the year practised by the Hungarian newcomers differed greatly from those practised by the Indo-European ethnic groups living in the same area, whose chief occupation was agriculture and who had already been partly converted to Christianity.

Medieval documents make particular reference to various games with horses and other sports and to the ritual sacrifice of a white horse. These traditions, however, were considered to be so "pagan" that their most striking elements (like animal sacrifice, for example) disappeared in the first centuries of Christianity, and were replaced by official church cere-monies.

It is most probable that the Magyar conquerors regarded spring or autumn as the beginning of the year. There are some related ethnic groups living in Asia today who still celebrate the beginning of the year in spring or autumn. In the case of nomadic tribes, the importance of these two seasons must have been increased by their habit of moving to special sum-mer pastures and then returning to the autumn and winter pastures in the settlement. Ninth-century Arab and Persian sources are known to have mentioned the nomadic way of life of the Hungarians who followed "grass and fertility".

Ibn Rusta (a lexicographer writing in Arabic in about the year 930) wrote the following about the Hungarians: "With the approach of the winter months they seek the shelter of the nearest river and stay there for the winter, fishing. This is the most suitable place for them to pass the winter."

There is still mention of this movement from one pasture to another in the legal documents of King László and King Kálmán and in the twelfth century, long after the Hungarians had settled in Central Europe. The memory of these ancient anniversaries has survived in the spring and autumn festivities practised by the shepherds, although they have taken on other characteristics in the thousand years that have elapsed, and have become more or less European.

WINTER CUSTOMS

We will begin our description of the Hungarian folk customs with the cycle of festivites held in the winter. This cycle contains a number of religious ceremonies (such as Christmas, Innocents's Day and Epiphany) that have their own characteristic features. The customs in the winter cycle do, however, possess a feature in common—they are all connected with the *beginning of the year*. St. Cathleen's Day, St. Andrew's Day, St. Barbara's Day and St. Lucy's Day celebrated at the end of November and the beginning of December, also point to the commencement of the year and herald its arrival.

The midwinter beginning of the year—Christmas and the New Year—(which corresponds more or less with the winter Solstice) was established and propagated by the Roman Empire at the same time that the computation of time according to the solar year was established. Many countries, however, did not accept the January 1st beginning of the year until a few centuries ago.

Up until the sixteenth century Christmas marked the beginning of the year in Hungary. The old Roman January 1st new year, however, was not forgotten in the civil life of the Middle Ages. Galeotto Marzio (1427–1497, a humanist and historian of Italian origin) noted that presents or *strenae* were distributed among the Hungarians in the court of Matthias Corvinus, King of Hungary (1440–1490), so that the year should begin well.

At the beginning of the sixteenth century, before the calendar reform, January 1st was still the occasion for giving new year presents in the Buda Court. The account books show entries of the amounts of money given on

III. "Busó" carnival in Mohács, Baranya County, 1970 ▶

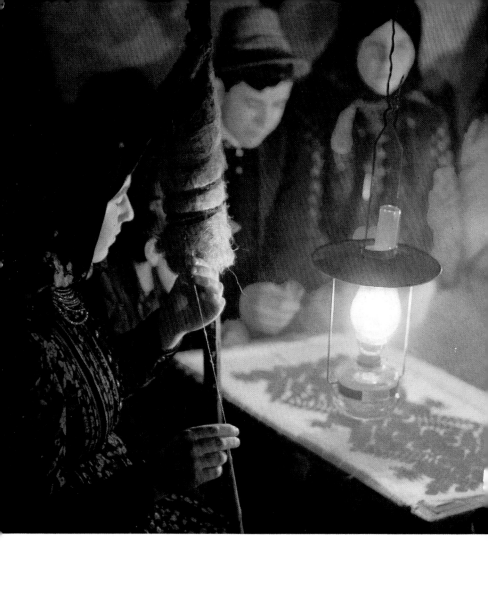

such occasions to school choirs who performed at the royal court, to cooks, soldiers, musicians (the zitherist and his dog, for example) and various craftsmen.

When the official date of the new year became January 1st, some of the old new year customs were transferred to this date, while the celebration of others remained at Christmas. Ever since then the weather for the following year is predicted, gifts are exchanged and season's greetings given both at Christmas time and at the New Year. **17**

The new year customs in many countries, including Hungary, developed mainly from a belief that during initial periods—in this case, the beginning of the year—completed actions analogically brought about later repetitions of the same actions. According to popular belief what happens on the first day of the year is bound to recur later. Consequently, in order to ensure good luck in the coming year, people try to perform as many pleasant deeds as possible—they join friends in new year merry-making beside tables loaded with food and wish one another the very best.

Apart from these intentional actions with their magic purpose, people try to predict from "accidental" occurrences. In the eighteenth century the great scholar Péter Bod, one of the pioneers in the history of Hungarian literature, wrote about the "onion or garlic calendar", which is made at New Year and used in the prediction of the weather for the coming twelve months. Salt is put into twelve cloves of garlic, with each clove representing one of the twelve months of the year. If the salt moistens in a particular clove by the morning, the month that it represents will be humid, will have rain or snow.

The casting of lead on New Year's Eve, the cooking of dumplings, performed by the girls, and the scattering of apple peel are also fortune-telling customs.

The well-known custom of bidding farewell to the old year is accompanied by wild vociferation and clangour. There are various possible local explanations for the motive behind the creation of so much noise. It could have been produced to drive away evil spirits, or the old year, or it could simply have been the general unrestrained gaiety of the new year festivity. Sometimes real epic legends are linked to this custom, in Hajdúszoboszló (a town on the Great Hungarian Plain), for example, I was told that the vociferation at the end of the year dated back to the wars against the Turks. On New Year's

◀ *IV. In the spinning room. Szék (Sic, Rumania), 1972*

Eve the women of the town beat tins together and rang the church bells in an effort to frighten the Turks away. Ever since then the last evening of each year is accompanied by a similar commotion.

18   People still firmly persist in the superstitious customs surrounding eating habits at the beginning of the year. In Hungary, for instance, pork must be eaten as it brings luck into the house; it is forbidden, on the other hand, to eat chicken, because it pecks good luck away. The songs of greeting and the good wishes that are delivered from door to door are also considered to have magic power. These expressions of goodwill can be given at any time during the midwinter festivites, from Christmas Eve to Epiphany. Some of the new year greetings that are popular today can be found in songbooks dating right back to the sixteenth century.

Christmas

Since the Magyar tribes first settled in Central Europe they were open to many influences which led to the development of the Hungarian Christmas customs. The Catholic religious rites and songs developed in this way during the Middle Ages as did the dramatic elements, like the Christmas plays and the custom of erecting a manger that were implanted by monks and teachers. Popular versions of these customs developed over the centuries.

Other rituals of a more magical character were also established in Hungary, like the ceremonial laying of the table at Christmas, the Christmas customs of strewing hay and of herdsmen carrying switches.

The Christmas tree first appeared in the towns in the 1840's and 50's, but has since spread throughout Hungary. Today Christmas trees are erected wherever there are children. In some counties of Transylvania, even during the Second World War, presents were brought for the children at New Year by the "golden foal".

The popular Nativity plays in Hungary are centred round amusing jokes, songs and acts performed by shepherds dressed in huge fur capes worn inside out. The Nativity players carry a home-made manger with them or a small house in the shape of a church *(Plates 6, 7 and I)*. Nowadays it is the children who perform the Nativity plays, except for one or two Székely villages in Transylvania, where grown-up men present the miracle plays, with the peculiar addition of formidable masks made of animal skins worn

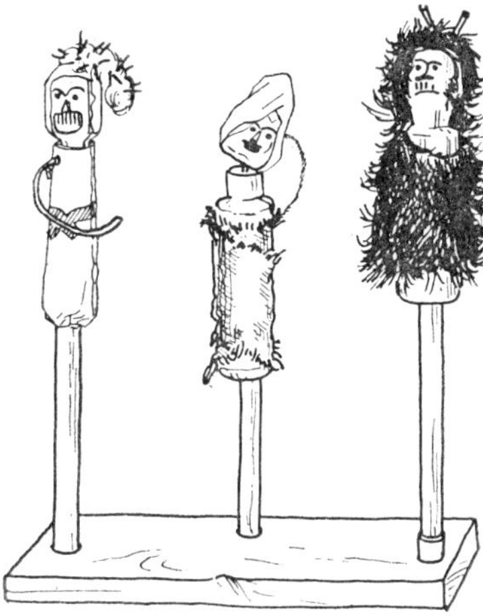

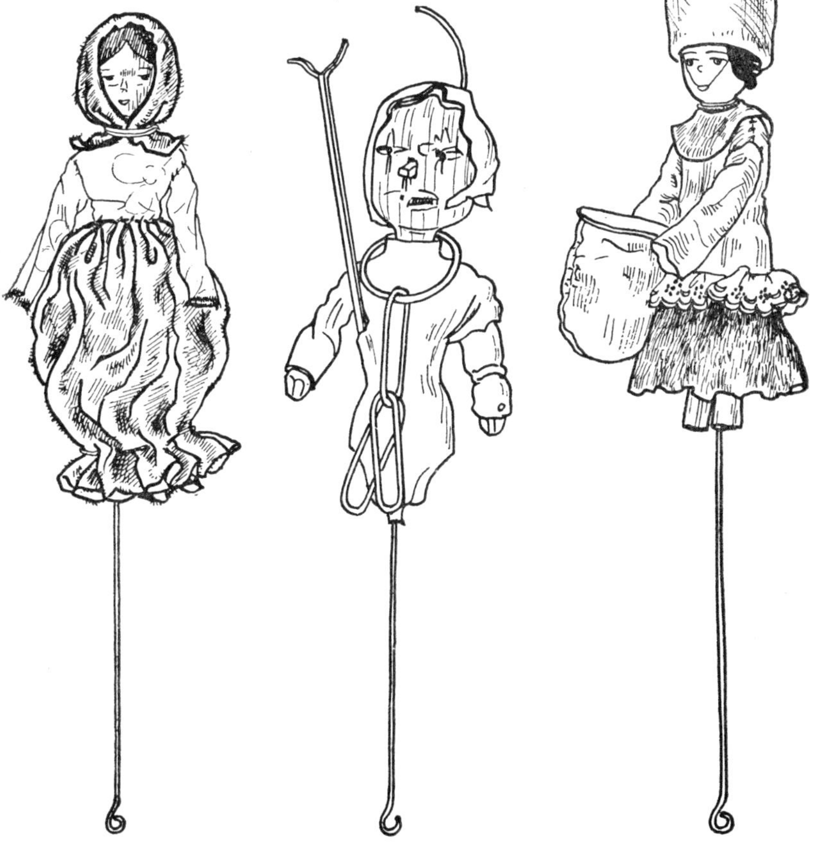

Puppets in the Nativity play

by shepherds. An example of this is the *Csobánolás* or Nativity play performed by the Székelys who moved from Bucovina (Rumania) in the 1940's and settled in Tolna County.

The oldest section of Christmas plays in this country are the Latin liturgical plays that were introduced in the eleventh century. No texts of medieval Hungarian Christmas plays have survived, but we can follow their development during the Baroque period. The records indicate that in the seventeenth and eighteenth centuries the plays were performed mostly by religious laymen and schoolchildren. From the nineteenth century onwards we know of two main types of Nativity plays—the play with actors and the play with puppets. The latter is known as the dancing puppet Nativity play and had two regional centres in Hungary, namely Transdanubia and the Upper Tisza region. Christmas puppet plays also occurred in other areas but only sporadically *(Plate 10)*.

The most important scene in the Hungarian Nativity play is the pastoral. The shepherds asleep in the pasture are awoken by the Angel, who sends them to the new-born baby, Jesus. The main character is a deaf old shepherd whose amusing misunderstandings form the chief source of humour. The other episodes in the play are as follows: the Holy Family are shown looking for shelter (here the play sometimes introduces the owner of a house refusing to give them accommodation, or the rich blacksmith's heartlessness and how he is punished for it); then the shepherds—occasionally accompanied by the Three Magi from the East—are represented taking presents to the Holy Child. Some scenes with Herod may also be included in the Nativity play, like, for example, Herod's meeting with the Three Magi from the Orient, Herod's counsel with his chief and so on. The scenes with Herod, however, can be presented as a separate play on Epiphany.

The dialogue of the Nativity plays has several regional versions. The Transylvanian plays are the oldest, with some scenes dating back to the seventeenth century. The Transdanubian Nativity plays have also preserved some archaisms, like the shepherd's names Titirus, Maksus, and Koridon that were fashionable in Baroque literary life.

The contrasts between good and evil, and rich and poor are depicted in the plays with great simplicity and expressiveness. The shepherds provide the humour when they misunderstand the Angel's Latin. They are ignorant but warm-hearted and gladly part with most of their small possessions.

Requests for donations or gifts bring the Nativity plays and other customs that take the form of plays to an end.

Besides the Nativity cycle other peasant miracle and morality plays were performed in certain areas. The Garden of Eden play, for example, tells the **21** story of the Fall of Adam and Eve.

The setting of the Christmas table was a particularly popular custom in the Catholic regions of the country. In Somogy County, for instance, the table was covered with hay, and various objects—combs, whetstones and knives—were placed on the corners. The table was then spread with a tablecloth. In the district of Zselicség three tablecloths were used and each one had to be placed on the table in an east-westerly direction. Oats, wheat and corn were mixed together in a bread basket, then various items of horse gear were placed on top and the basket was put under the table.

In many parts of the country herdsmen used to carry switches to the houses at Christmas time. This custom, which was considered to have magic power, was observed in the villages beside the river Ipoly, for example. During the Christmas fast, cowherds carrying bundles of sticks used to visit all the houses where cows were kept. The women at each house took as many switches from the bundle as they had cows and then hit the cowherd's legs with them. The carrying of switches was usually accompanied by expressions of goodwill.

Nativity masks worn by the Székelys from **Bukovina**

Wassailing (regölés)

This is the Hungarian version of the Christmas and new year custom of
wassailing that is practised throughout most of Europe. On such occasions
children, young men or adult men go from one house to another wishing
wealth and happiness in the coming year *(Plate 11)*. Although this custom
is so widely known, its name in this country is very old and very Hungarian.
According to linguists, the Hungarian word for wassailing—"regölés"—just
like the refrain in the "regös" or wassailing song ("Hej, regö rejtem...") is
Finno-Ugrian in origin, and is linked to the oldest examples of Hungarian
poetry and popular beliefs. The word has also kept the memory of the ancient shamanistic songs alive.

Medieval documents often refer to "the regös" by name, meaning min-
strels at festivities and royal drinking parties, or combibators, to use the Latin
expression. The first Monday after Epiphany was termed Wassailing Monday in the calendars from the sixteenth to the eighteenth century. The
Transylvanian prose writer Gáspár Heltai, living in the sixteenth century,
mentioned wassailing week as a time when people drank and revelled, in
what he considered the Devil's Festival. Historical documents refer to the
act of wassailing and to the wassailers, but no records of the texts of the old
wassailing songs have been found.

In the last two centuries wassailing has been practised in Transdanubia
and in Udvarhely County in Transylvania. The young men of Transdanubia
equipped with sticks fitted with chains and home-made musical instruments
(e.g. a pot with a hog's bladder stretched over the top and a stick through it)
used to visit the houses where the girls were of marriageable age and sing
magic songs. One definite incentive for these incantations was to charm the
house with fecundity—to wish the people in the house good health and for-
tune. In the second part of the song the wassailers bewitched a girl by singing about her and linking her with one particular boy. The extent to which
this was taken seriously can still be proved today. In December 1968 I asked
two elderly people from the village of Egyházasfalu (Győr-Sopron County)
if I could make a recording of them singing a wassailing song. They gave
their consent willingly, but before beginning they spent some time considering which girl's and boy's name should be mentioned in the song, for fear
of bewitching a badly matched couple.

These two sections of the song are preceded by an opening speech in which the wassailers claim that they have come on a long, tiring journey and that they are not robbers, but the servants of King Stephen. The reason for this is that the most important date for wassailing was December 26th, the **23** Day of Stephen the Protomartyr, and his figure merged in the minds of the ordinary people with Stephen, the first king of Hungary.

A section dealing with the magic stag is also part of the introduction. According to the song, an expanse of pure, fresh water appears surrounded by grass, on which the young magic stag is grazing. The candles on the thousand branches of the stag's antlers alight without being lit and die without being quenched. The stag appears in other songs with the moon, sun or stars depicted on his body.

Many experts have tried to solve the puzzle surrounding the mythical stag. One known fact is that the stag appears in the legends of the North American Indians and many European and Asian peoples as a symbol of the starry sky, especially the winter sky. This song must therefore be a mythical representation of the winter Solstice, indicating the recurring seasons.

God rest you merry gentlemen! We are the wassailers.
Yonder where the stream appears
My sheep are grazing.
Enchanted Stag!
Antlers with a thousand branches,
On each branch a thousand candles,
Blaze in splendour,
Flicker and die,
Sing hey, sing ho,
A-wassailing we go.
Here they are calling
A pretty girl
Whose name is
Frances Német,
Sing hey, sing ho,
A-wassailing we go.

The wassailers' musical instrument

Yonder they are calling
A handsome boy
Whose name is
Mihály Varga,
Sing hey, sing ho,
A-wassailing we go.

Our greetings to the master
And his good wife,
Sing hey, sing ho,
A-wassailing we go.

The bag lies in the corner
Full of forint notes,
Half for the master,
Half for we who sing,
Sing hey, sing ho,
A-wassailing we go.

Our robes are of oakwood, our sandals of greenwood. Now we must be on our way, no joke! Get ourselves some baccy for a smoke. So goodnight, goodnight!

(The village of Egyházasfalu in Győr-Sopron County)

The "hey-ho" chanters

The custom of "hey-ho" chanting in West Transdanubia is very similar to the New Year's Eve "hey-ho" chanting performed by the most easterly group of Hungarian speaking people—the Csángós of Moldavia (Rumania). The purpose of their custom was to ensure the continued success in the new year of the "magic" process in which wheat became bread. The name of this custom ("hey-ho" chant) shows linguistic similarity with the refrain of the wassailing song (Sing hey, sing ho...). Among the many noisy instruments used during wassailing and "hey-ho" chanting, the "bull" was very popular. It consisted of a piece of bark with skin stretched over it and horse-

V. Mummery on Shrove Tuesday. Moha, Fejér County, 1970 ▶

hair attached to the middle. By running the fingers down the horsehair a bull-like roar could be produced.

"Hey-ho" chanting still took place in the fifties in some Moldavian villages. The performers were young men who went chiefly to the houses where **25** unmarried girls lived. The songs were accompanied by the cracking of whips and the sound of bells, pipes, drums and the "bull" instrument. The "hey-ho" chant relates the story of the wheat from the sowing of the seed to the baking of bread. The Moldavian Rumanians greet the new year with a similar text. The words of their song are roughly as follows: the servants set out with twelve pairs of oxen and twelve ploughs. They go to the fields to plough and sow the fine wheat. When the wheat is ripe, sickles are made and the wheat is harvested. The servants take the wheat to the mill where the miller grinds it and then the farmer's wife bakes a milk loaf from the golden flour and gives it to the "hey-ho" chanters. The refrain is repeated after each verse and accompanied by the ringing of bells and cracking of whips.

Name-day celebrations

The name-days for Stephen and John are celebrated on December 26th and 27th in the Hungarian villages. As a result of the great popularity of these two names, the celebrations on December 26th and 27th have come to be regarded as an important part of the Christmas cycle of festivities. Stephen and John name-days are occasions when friends celebrate together and acquaintances pay their respects, and as both days are holidays, visitors are welcome to partake in the feast.

One interesting motive of the Stephen and John name-day greetings is the story of the "tree growing in paradise". This particular story, which is reminiscent of the Fall of Adam and Eve, must have originally been part of the Christmas fast ceremony. The congratulatory songs on Stephen and John name-days call to mind the Root of Jesse, or rather Christ's Descent. These particular name-day songs are good examples of how old religious and mythical songs and incantations are transformed into mere poetic motives with aesthetic designs.

◄ *VI. Easter sprinkling. Acsa, Pest County, 1971*

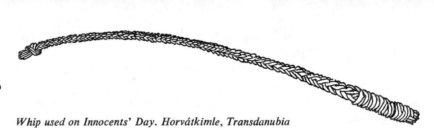

Whip used on Innocents' Day. Horvátkimle, Transdanubia

Innocents' Day

The custom of whipping on December 28th is known throughout Hungary. The blessing of whips on Innocents' Day originally formed part of the church ceremonies in the fifteenth and sixteenth centuries. Pelbárt Temesvári, a famous fifteenth-century preacher, often spoke about Hungarian folk customs in his sermons. In his Innocents' Day sermon, he rebuked those who converted church traditions into abusive jokes: "Why is it, my friends, that there are many among you today who indulge in idle jocularity and whip one another, chanting that Herod slaughtered many children in Bethlehem, David's City? Such individuals are introducing many bad elements, sinful behaviour, may indeed, improper fondling and other unmentionable actions into this custom." In the sixteenth century the Hungarian students in Cracow were often punished for this custom.

The "Innocents, David, David!" song is still accompanied today by whipping. In Jászság and other regions of Hungary performers ask on such occasions how many innocents there are. During the whipping they chant a song to drive sores and illnesses away:

> *Be dutiful and good*
> *If they send you down, you should go up,*
> *If they send you up, you should go down,*
> *If they send you for water, bring wine,*
> *If they send you for wine, bring water,*
> *Be healthy, be nimble, but don't have boils.*

(Zalaistvánd)

The whipping on Innocents' Day is one of the most significant customs in Transdanubia during the winter season. In some villages in Somogy County whipping begins on St. Nicholas' Day and continues until new year. In Győr-Sopron County the custom of whipping is linked with the young men's *coming of age*. This is the Hungarian version of the initiation ceremony. December 28th was not the only day for the coming-of-age ceremony as it could be coupled with any other custom during the year in which young men played the main role, like the wassailing custom, for example.

In Dunaremete the coming-of-age ceremony is preceded by whipping. The young men go round to all the houses where the girls live and sing beautiful old songs while they "beat" each member of the family with their whips. The girls tie ribbons to the whips and their mothers give wrapped-up pieces of meat to the group. The boys then proceed to a tavern and cook the meat they have collected on an open fire. When the meat has been eaten the initiation can begin. The ceremony itself, in which only men participate, is introduced by a long speech, in which the story of the slaughter of the children in Bethlehem is linked with the coming of age. When the speech is over, the godfather pours a glass of wine over each boy and everyone joins in a drinking bout. The tipsy young men are then taken to one or two of the families with marriageable daughters, where they are received by the mothers and daughters with amused forbearance, and helped over the difficult and embarrassing visit. This visit brings a great ceremonial turning point in their lives to a close.

The coming-of-age ceremony in this form can only be found today on the Little Plain in Hungary, although similar festivites were once held on Innocents' Day in Brassó (Braşov, Rumania) and in many Székely regions in East Transylvania. In Méra, for example, the young men had to spend the night preceding the ceremony in the spinning-house. It was here that the drinking speer was held, and no one was allowed to enter the house. The next morning the boys visited the girls and hit them with sticks chanting at the same time "Innocents, David, David!" If a girl was fond of a boy she offered him food and was then escorted by him to the spinning-house for the dance, which began at dawn.

28 The Hungarian word *Vízkereszt* is a loan translation from the Greek *Hagiasmos*, whereas most Catholic countries adopted the Greek "Epiphania" or the equivalent of the "Day of the Three Magi". (We know from an eleventh-century ecclesiastical document that the Greek form of the Epiphany festival was practised in Hungary.)

Foreign visitors in the fifteenth century spoke of the priests' collection of alms on Twelfth-day as a feature peculiar to Hungary. The benediction of the houses was also held on January 6th, when the first letter of the names of each of the Three Magi were written on the door.

The "carrying of the star" and the singing of the "star song" have been recognized traditions since the sixteenth century. In some parts of Hungary, children still go round the village in threes, representing the Magi and carrying a star sceptre. The "star song" and the Twelfth-day play are sometimes performed by girls *(Plates 12, 13)*.

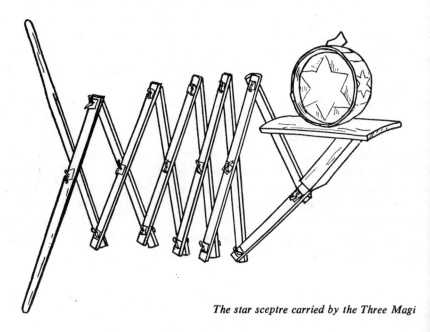

The star sceptre carried by the Three Magi

Carnival

Historical records contain more information about the carnival festivities than about any other tradition, because both church and secular authorities condemned the custom as too noisy and disturbing, and forbade its practice. The carnival survived, however, despite this, and is performed today with exactly the same amount of zest.

The most striking feature of the carnival cycle of festivities in Hungary and in other European countries is the masked mummery. Documents first mentioned the exchange of clothes between men and women, the wearing of masks and the various forms of animal disguises in the fifteenth century. The carnival was performed everywhere in Hungary from the sovereign's court to the smallest village. During the reign of King Matthias (1458–1490) the Italian relatives of his wife, Queen Beatrix, used to send beautifully made masks as presents to their Hungarian relations.

In the sixteenth and seventeenth centuries people in the villages, towns and the king's court wore masks during the carnival season activities. Great carnivals are known to have taken place in the court of the ill-fated King Louis II up until the battle of Mohács in 1526, when the Turks waged a decisive attack against the Hungarians and King Louis was killed. Elephant-mummery took part in the great carnival held in the king's court on Shrove Tuesday in 1525. King Louis himself also appeared during the festivities wearing a devil's mask. The amusing contest between Sour Soup and Broth, or rather Lenten Fare and Meat Dish is mentioned from the sixteenth century onwards. This contest was rendered as a play in several countries of Europe, and in Transylvania reference is made to the humorous combat performed with straw puppets and still held in this century.

Masked carnival parades can still be found in the villages of Hungary today *(Plate V)*. While the carnival masquerades of some European countries form mass processions, the mummery of smaller masked groups is more popular in Hungary. The most spectacular parade of the carnival season in this country is the "busó" procession performed by the Southern Slavs living in Mohács. The participants appear in carved wooden masks and follow a ritual pattern of movement and behaviour. The "busó" masks were originally worn by "Sokác" men only, for the boys and men from other villages had a different guise *(Plates 14, 15, 16, 17 and III)*.

A carnival mask made of rags

The animal masks in the village processions are particularly striking. Bear, horse, goat and stork disguises are the most popular among the mummers. The players generally perform short dialogues—an owner takes his horse or goat to market, for example, and while he is bargaining the animal collapses and dies, but is brought to life again at the sound of music.

Other disguises apart from the animal masks are also worn during the village carnival. These masks, unlike the grotesque wooden "busó" ones, are usually made from stockings, rags, or paper *(Plates 18 and 19)*. The robber, gypsy woman, bride and bridegroom or old man and old woman with a baby are some of the traditional fancy dresses. Comic funerals and mock weddings are also performed during the carnival season.

The most striking of the carnival marriages is the mock wedding ceremony in Transdanubia, where the "newly-weds" are carried through the village on a log *(Plate 20)*. I took part in one of these amusing ceremonies in the village of Rábatótfalu in 1968. The men cut down a tree 31 metres high, and a young couple sat upon it and were pulled along the main road by the other boys and girls from Szentgotthárd to Rábatótfalu. There were 168 people taking part in the procession, all in fancy dress; apart from the "brides" and "bridegrooms" some were dressed as wedding guests, others as devils, gypsies, clowns or craftsmen. The carnival parade was interrupted twice for the farcical wedding ceremony to take place. Mock weddings and the pulling of the log are performed in those years when no marriages take place in the village. Some years ago unmarried girls in many parts of the country had to pull a log on Shrove Tuesday.

It was once customary to hold special parades during the carnival season for women and girls only. The Palots (a North Hungarian ethnic group) living in the Karancs Mountain region, used to hold a "girls' Sunday" a week before Carnival Sunday. After dinner on Sunday the girls went round the village carrying sticks and singing greetings. Their songs were religious and comprised requests for donations. The round of visits was followed by dancing in the evening.

Pelbárt Temesvári, the fifteenth-century preacher mentioned before, already knew of the existence of these special carnivals for women. In one of his sermons he wrote about the women in a village near Kapos, who dressed up as men or wore other disguises and danced and sang until the devil **31** himself appeared, seized one of them and flung her into the Kapos swamp.

Such carnivals still occasionally take place today. In 1968 the women of Mátraalmás paraded round the village in fancy dress and "shaved" the men with icicles. A ball was then held in the evening at which men were forbidden to attend.

The ideas behind the carnival were usually connected with marriage. At the end of the carnival season it was customary to ridicule the girls who were still unmarried. On Shrove Tuesday in Szatmár, for example, the boys used to clang pieces of tin together just below the windows of single girls and shout:

> *If you have a grown-up daughter*
> *Pack her off to the fields.*

St. Blaze's Day and St. Gregory's Day

St. Blaze's Day which falls on February 3rd and St. Gregory's Day on March 12th were school festivities. The ceremonies on St. Gregory's Day were the most widespread. The day marked the end of the winter term at school. On such occasions the school children paraded round in fancy dress and asked for donations. The collections made on both days often insured the emoluments of the teacher.

Some of the songs written in a mixture of Latin and Hungarian for these occasions have survived from the seventeenth and eighteenth centuries, as teachers and school children carefully wrote down the songs they sang during the collections.

The celebrations on both occasions took on the form of plays. On St. Gregory's Day one able boy was appointed to play the role of Pope Gregory, while the other children followed behind in procession, dressed as bishops and soldiers. The older children encouraged the younger ones, who were not yet at school, to start learning. The most popular song performed during the procession of St. Gregory has survived to this day in the minds of the country folk. Apart from emphasizing the necessity to attend school, the song also refers to the arrival of spring.

> *On the day of our dear Saint Gregory, learned teacher,*
> *As of ancient time, God draws us in to school,*
> *See now how the birds are gathering and will come*
> *To greet the rosy dawn in joyful song.*

SPRING CUSTOMS

The spring customs can be divided into two large groups—the cycle of events during Easter Week and Whitsun.

The custom of throwing a straw dummy into the brook on Palm Sunday was popular in Hungary, while neighbouring countries in the north and west practised the same custom on other fasting Sundays. In some Palots villages this tradition still existed in the 1950's. The straw dummy was dressed in women's clothes, carried round the village, then destroyed and thrown into the water or burned *(Plate 21)*. People in countries west of Hungary regarded the dummy as a symbol of death or winter. The throwing of the dummy into a brook also had magic properties in this country, although the songs linked to it were of a rather jocular nature, referring to the fact that the fast was rapidly drawing to a close in the Catholic villages and that Lenten fare would soon be replaced by richer food and ham.

> *Go! Soup, go!*
> *Come! Ham, come!*

The custom of throwing straw dummies into water in the Hungarian villages in the Nyitra region (Czechoslovakia) was followed by the gathering of weeping willow branches. The village girls decorated the branches and carried them from house to house, hastening the departure of winter and welcoming the spring.

The *sprinkling of water* and the *painting of eggs* are the two most popular Easter customs. Both traditions are still practised in the villages and towns of Hungary today, with no sign of a depreciation in their popularity *(Plates 22, 23 and VI)*. One noticeable difference in the sprinkling custom is that,

VII. A girl carrying her Easter dish. Csököly, Somogy County, 1970 ►

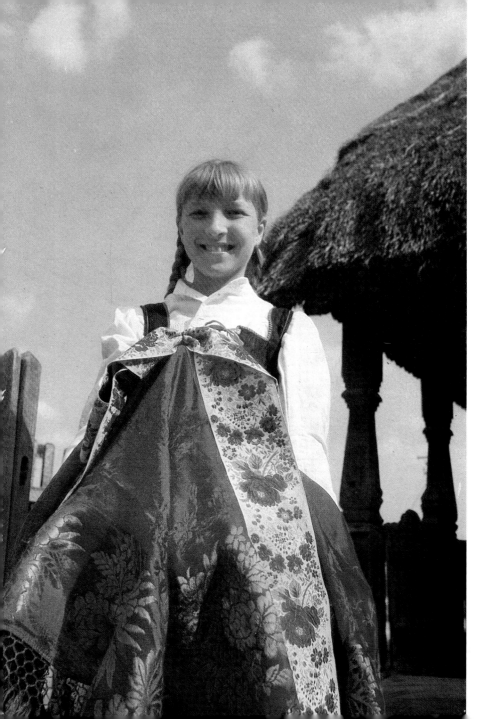

whereas years ago the girls were sprinkled with water from a well, they are now doused with scented water. (Whipping has replaced sprinkling at Easter in some villages that were probably Slovak in origin but are now Hungarian.) The object of both sprinkling and whipping was to achieve **33** ritual purification and fertility. Quite a lot is known about the past of Easter sprinkling. The expressions "water-taking Monday" and "water-throwing Tuesday" were used in the Middle Ages. The custom of painting eggs and the games connected with it are also very old. "Dies concussionis ovorum" (1380), the name for the first Monday after Low Sunday, refers to these games.

The egg is the symbol of fertility in most countries of Europe and Asia. The remains of eggs and painted egg shells have often been found in the burial places of the Avars and in tombs dating from the Migration Period.

The women and girls are responsible for decorating the eggs *(Plate 23)*. The easiest method of doing this is to stick leaves on to the shell and then dip the egg into paint. When the leaves are removed an attractive, crenated pattern remains. Not so long ago home-made paints were used by extracting the juice from onions, the green shell of walnuts, and from the peel of wild pears, crab-apples and oak-apples. A Moldavian woman living in the village of Egyházaskozár once told me in her quaint dialect that the women in the village generally used the cooked peel of crab-apples which turned the egg a gorgeous yellow. She also said that they sometimes drew patterns on the shell with wax and then dipped the egg in red paint.

The method of melting wax and then drawing patterns on the egg-shell with it is the most popular form of egg decoration. When the wax has set, the egg is dipped into paint and put aside until the wax peels off, leaving a yellowish-white pattern, which is sometimes painted in another colour.

Another way of decorating eggs is to scratch patterns on the surface with a sharp instrument. Even greater skill is required for the custom of decorating the egg with a horseshoe.

Some of the designs on the eggs have regional names. Egg painters will immediately recognize certain symmetrical or stylized motives. The characteristic designs on the Somogy County eggs, for example, are called sunflower seed, frogs' legs, butterfly on a reed, etc.

The killing of the cock was a recognized Easter tradition in Transylvania. In the village of Apáca this custom was still practised in the 1950's by small

◄ *VII. Carrying the Easter dish. Csököly, Somogy County, 1970*

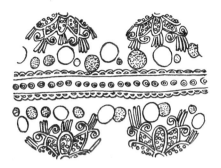

An Easter egg decorated with a horseshoe

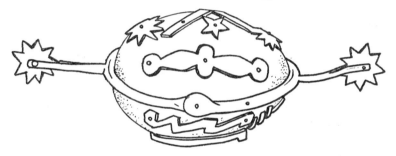

boys. Old-fashioned bows and arrows were used to kill the cock. Originally a live cock was used, but later on it was replaced by a board with a cock painted on it. The performers used to begin by surrounding the cock and singing a farewell chant. During the actual archery amusing rhymes were said but as soon as an arrow penetrated the cock's heart the game was over. The custom finished with consuming the cock soup.

The other group of Easter folk traditions developed from ecclesiastical rites. In the twelfth century the blessing of fire was already part of the ceremonies on Holy Saturday. Fire and water still play significant roles in the folk traditions and popular beliefs connected with Easter Week. The blessing of fire was customary in the Catholic villages. The noisy custom of "beating Pilate" during Holy Week was practised by the children. Walking round the fields is another century-old custom, which was linked in Zalaegerszeg with a historical legend of the Turkish wars.

The sending of Easter dishes

Easter dishes were usually sent on Low Sunday, the first Sunday after Easter. They usually contained food and drink and were exchanged between young girls as a sign of long-lasting friendship *(Plates VII and VIII)*. This custom is still practised in some regions of the country, particularly in the counties of Somogy and Zala in Transdanubia. The Easter or Sisterhood dish was generally sent from one girl to another. Occasionally boys would exchange dishes, or girls would send them to boys. The senders of Easter dishes accepted each other in true brotherhood and swore to remain faithful friends until death. From then on the formal way of greeting was adopted.

The contents of each dish varied, but Easter eggs, a milk loaf and a small bottle of wine or some other drink were always included. According to custom, the receiver of such a gift replaced one Easter egg from the dish with two of his own before returning it to the sender. In other regions the whole dish was exchanged for another one. The bestowing of the gift was accompanied by special greetings that were either sung or spoken. In Kéthely the following verse was recited:

This Easter dish of mine
With flowers of spring I twine,

> *Friend to friend*
> *This token send,*
> *Love's knot to tie,*
> *Or else deny.*

The following verse comes from Szentmihályhegy:

> *Loved one, loved one we are joined*
> *Till death betwixt us come,*
> *If you deceive me, if you beat me,*
> *We shall still be bound as one.*

This short verse was heard in Göcsej:

> *Loved one, loved one we are sworn*
> *to stay together till the final morn.*

In Baranya County the poem recited by boys and girls to their chosen friend went like this:

> *In my gilded dish*
> *Easter gifts I bring.*
> *Virgin to virgin offered,*
> *Friend to friend proffered.*
> *If it be not to your pleasure*
> *Take no blame!*
> *Home again I'll take my treasure*
> *By the way I came.*

The Csángós of Moldavia combined the sending of Easter eggs with the exchange of dishes on the first Sunday after Easter. The girls who performed this custom were bound together in lifelong friendship. In some parts of the country, the tradition of sending gifts also occurred in conjunction with other festivities, on any day from Low Sunday to Midsummer day. Sándor Réső Ensel wrote about the custom in 1867, practised at Whitsun by the girls of Eger. In Gyöngyös, at the turn of the century, Whitsun was the time when young men sent dishes to their sweethearts. Instead of Easter dishes, attractively decorated branches were exchanged by the girls of some villages in Baranya County.

Games

The games for boys and girls were once performed on the Sundays between Easter and Whitsun. I was told the following about the games in Földes (Hajdú-Bihar County): "From Easter to Whitsun whatever the weather, even if it snowed, the peasant boys used to put on their wide linen trousers. Their trousers were made from three widths of material gathered at the waist. The boys and girls used to march out of the village in separate groups to the meadow nearby, singing as they went. It was here that the games began. They either played ball games, tag, or blind-man's-buff. The older boys, those who were shortly getting married, remained in a separate group throughout. This was how the games were played."

These games performed by boys and girls from Easter to Whitsuntide were customary in other areas of Hungary too. The "White Lily" game was played after litany in the villages of Zala County, from Easter Monday to Whit Monday. Those taking part joined hands and played singing games. Among the various games was one entitled "Grow, grow, green branch", in which two girls joined hands and raised their arms up high to form an arch for the others to pass under one by one. This game is very similar to the English game Oranges and Lemons. Another traditional game is the "White Lily" game, the song of which goes like this:

Leap into the Danube
White Madonna Lily,
Cling to the staff of gold,
Wash you, dry you
on the golden kerchief.

With the disappearance of this custom, games like "Grow, grow, green branch" developed into children's singing games that were not attached to any particular occasion. Most spring songs speak of love. Here are the words of one which was sung for me by a woman of Moldavian origin:

O'er the lake the Spring wind blows,
Flower o' mine, flower o' mine,
Every bird its true love knows,
Flower o' mine, flower o' mine. **39**
Who then shall I choose for mate,
Flower o' mine, flower o' mine?
You and I should share our fate,
Flower o' mine, flower o' mine.
I plucked a blossom from my garden,
Frail and lovely gilly-flower.
I plucked a blossom from my garden,
Frail and lovely gilly-flower.
On her white legs the turtle dove
Steps among the gilly-flowers.
Her legs are white, her wings are green,
Oh how soft she beats them.

(Egyházaskozár, 1967)

St. George's Day

This was a great festive occasion in Hungary; in the minds of the ordinary people it had the same significance as May 1st had in neighbouring western countries. It was the spring day of evil pursuits, when witches were free to do mischief. People used to fix thorny and birch branches on the fences and front doors of their houses to ward off evil spirits. During the ancient trials for witchcraft mention was always made of St. George's Day as the day when the witch's power was the greatest. It was believed that if you walked to the crossroads on St. George's Day you would see the witches, who had been up since dawn collecting dew in the meadows. They collected the dew in large sheets which were later wrung out and the moisture given to the cows to drink. In other regions it was popular belief that the witches stole the "goodness" from the wheat when they took the dew away. During their pranks, the witches chanted "I gather, gather, only half I gather", in the hope that no one would notice the loss and that their wickedness would remain a secret.

I heard the following mythical legend from a woman in Jászság in 1957: "My grandmother told me this story," she began, "about a young married couple who were very poor and had to share a kitchen with an old woman. **40** One day the two women decided to bake bread together and they set to work, kneading the dough in two separate bowls. The same quantity of flour had been used by both, but when the bread was done, the old woman's had risen into two beautiful big loaves, while the young woman had only made one very small loaf. The girl asked her husband to find out how the old woman had done it, so he went to her and said: 'Dear old lady, please tell me how you baked your bread?' 'How I bake my bread? But you saw how it was made, with flour, my son, ordinary flour!' 'No, it wasn't,' cried the young man, 'only one loaf can be made from that quantity of dough.' 'Oh the devil take you and your questions! But, if you really want to know, come with me to the Trinity crossroad tonight, at the stroke of midnight. I shall then draw a circle and you must stand in the middle, and stay there whatever approaches you, be it a fiery bull, a wild animal, a lion, or the devil himself. You must not tread out of the circle on any account.' So they met at midnight and made their way to the crossroads, where the old woman drew a circle. All sorts of strange figures and animals leaped round the young man and frightened him terribly, but he remained in the circle and came to no harm. When the old woman returned she said: 'Now I see, you have stood the test and are beginning to understand me.' Some hours later the young man returned, as the woman had instructed, bringing a sheet that he and his wife had woven. The two of them then set out for the meadows and walked across the corn fields dragging the sheet over the dew-covered wheat. As they pulled the sheet they chanted: 'I gather, gather, only half I gather.' 'If we had said, I gather it all,' the old woman explained, 'the wheat crop would have been completely destroyed.' As it was, they only spoiled half the crop.

"But to go on with the story, when the sheet was soaked with dew the boy and the old woman took it home and squeezed all the liquid into a bowl. And from then on whenever they baked bread a spoonful of dew was added to the flour and the loaves rose big and beautiful. They had taken half the farmer's wheat crop and increased their own amount of bread many times over. That is how a lot of bread can be made from a little dough. When the young wife made her bread in the same way, it was discovered that she too was endowed with magic power."

IX. The maypole. Somogy County, 1970 ▶

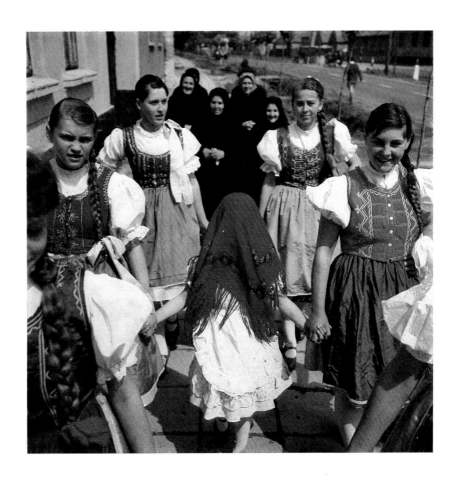

St. George's Day was also the first and most important day of the year for cattle to be driven to pasture. (This was, however, sometimes carried out on other days—Maundy Thursday or Good Friday.) It was the custom on such occasions to perform magic actions in an attempt to protect the cattle while they were grazing. In the region of Zala a chain was attached to the inside of the cowshed door and eggs were placed outside before the cattle were allowed to come out. It was believed that each cow would be charmed as it moved past the chain and eggs on its way to pasture, and would grow as strong as the chain and as round as an egg. **41**

May Day

Houses were decorated with leafy branches on the first day of May as early as the fifteenth century. In one of his sermons Pelbárt Temesvári referred to this custom as being connected in some way with the martyrdom of the two apostles Philip and Jacob, but later he added that the explanation was more likely to be found in the fact that on May Day since time immemorial men had been filled with wonder at the fragrance of the green meadows and shady forests and at the beauty of the birds' singing. Jacob-tree or Jacob-branch are the East Transylvanian names for the maypole, elsewhere it is called dawn-tree or maypole.

The erection of the maypole is known throughout the country *(Plate IX)*. The Lutherans used to put up the maypole in the church as well. This custom was denounced by Sámuel Tessedik in 1774. It was generally the boys who erected the maypole for the girls. Years ago boys usually stole a tree for the purpose and it was because of this that the custom was so often forbidden by the authorities. But the official regulation had no real effect, as the young men still managed to produce maypoles from somewhere and show the village which girls they were courting. The maypole in Jászság is usually a poplar and is decorated with crêpe paper and ribbons. Bottles of wine and other gifts are also put on the tree. In the Palots region the young man used to erect the maypole and the girl and her mother would decorate it. The "dancing out" of the maypole was performed in many villages at Whitsun or at the end of May; this meant that the maypole was ceremoniously broken up accompanied by music and dancing. Today the favourite teacher in the village or the president of the local county council also receives a maypole.

◄ *X. The Whitsun Queen's parade. Vitnyéd, Győr-Sopron County, 1970*

The sending of flowers in May is a new version of this custom, introduced recently. I had the opportunity to observe the new procedure in the township of Gyöngyöspata. Instead of erecting maypoles the boys sent decorated pots of flowers to the girls, who placed them in the window. The flowers showed the village inhabitants the serious intentions of a boy in just the same way as the maypole once did.

The first May Day procession was organized in 1890 by Hungarian factory workers. A detailed account of this can be found in the first volume of *Ethnographia*. During the inter-war period miners from the region of Salgótarján used to organize outings and dances on May Day in secret. Excursions and meetings are still arranged today in memory of these occasions in the forests surrounding the town.

Whitsun King and Queen

There are many extant historical documents that throw light on the past of this custom of choosing a Whitsun King. In the sixteenth century, insignificant, temporary power was called "Whitsun royalty". We can suppose that the custom was known in this country many years before that. According to historical documents from the sixteenth to the nineteenth century, Whitsun Kings were mostly chosen during some kind of competition. North Hungarian synodical regulations repeatedly forbade the ancient custom of choosing a Whitsun King and dancing on Whit Sunday. These interdictions show that the custom was popular with Hungarians and Slovaks alike.

In his study of the region of Csallóköz, in 1736, the geographer Mátyás Bél mentioned a village called Szent Örzsébet (St. Elizabeth), which was visited on Whit Sunday by Hungarian pilgrims who then chose a Whitsun King following the ancient custom. The reference to this village is very interesting because the name St. Elizabeth often appears in Whitsun songs today. Mór Jókai, the great Hungarian romantic novelist of the last century, described a horse race in chapter eight of his novel *A Hungarian Nabob*, in which a Whitsun King was selected. When the chosen king was not accepted by the spectators the competitors had to fight a wild bull. All sorts of competitions of skill were organized to decide who would be Whitsun King; the children of Transylvania took part in tug of war contests, in other areas goose decapitation games were organized and so on.

Since the beginning of the twentieth century the choosing of Whitsun Kings by contest has disappeared. The last vestiges of this old custom were recorded some decades ago in West Transdanubia, where the children used to cover themselves with leaves and masquerade at Whitsuntide. In the village **43** of Sopronhorpács they called this practice the dance of the Turkish pasha and related historical legends about it.

Another form of this tradition was discovered at the end of the eighteenth century. A boy and a girl were selected from the village to be king and queen, and then paraded round the village adorned with flowers. In other regions of Hungary small children were chosen as the Whitsun pair.

One of the folk customs still alive today in Transdanubia is the walk of the Whitsun Queen performed by girls. The little Queen's companions hold a silk scarf like a canopy over her head *(Plate X)*, and in this manner they go from one house to another offering their best wishes and scattering rose petals on the ground *(Plate 24)*. The Queen must remain silent throughout this procedure and must not smile when people try to provoke her. The aim behind this magic ritual is to promote the growth of flax. At each house the girls lift the Queen high in the air and chant: "This is how high flax must grow!" The girls receive presents for their good wishes.

The relation between these traditions is not clear. The Central European custom of selecting a Whitsun King during horse racing events and other contents probably replaced the ancient spring rituals performed by the Hungarian pagans. (It is interesting to note that the Mongolians still hold similar horse races and sport events for the lads in spring.) The Transdanubian custom of masquerading in a covering of leaves was most likely a magic ritual to bring on rain. In Transdanubia Whitsun was also the day for cleaning out the well.

The songs that accompany the Whitsun traditions, particularly those in which St. Elizabeth's name is mentioned, are very interesting. This connection must come from the fact that the peony flower (in Hungarian Whitsun rose), is often referred to in the songs, and in the legend of St. Elizabeth the rose also plays an important part. The miracle of the rose is one of the main episodes in the legend, in which Elizabeth takes alms in secret to the poor. On one occasion she is stopped and questioned but nothing can be proved, for the bread in her apron turns into roses. This series of songs, which were probably once much more closely related than they are now, contain many different elements. They refer to a mysterious being who was created on a rose-tree and to the Whitsun horse races, apart from the well-wishing and requests for alms:

Of no earthly mother was I born,
But from a rose-tree on Whitsun morn.

*

What day, what day's today? Red Whitsun day.
Tomorrow, yes, tomorrow is the second day.
Good lasses and lads, take pains,
Hold tightly the horse's reins,
On the sweet peony red
Beware you trample not, nor tread.

SUMMER CUSTOMS

The lighting of St. John's Fire

The ritual tradition of lighting fires was usually held in Hungary on the eve of June 24th. Fires were ceremoniously lit on other occasions too—during the Christmas fast, at carnival time and at Easter—but their popularity was nothing compared to the lighting of fires during summer Solstice. The custom was widely practised in the sixteenth century; but today it is rapidly disappearing, although it can still be found in one or two villages in Somogy County and in Hungarian-speaking areas beyond the Hungarian border. During the inter-war period the custom was still practised in places along the Galga and Ipoly rivers.

An interesting question arises here, as to whether the religious custom of lighting John the Baptist's Fire replaced an original ritual by fire, performed by the pagan Magyars. We know that Ibn Rusta referred to the Hungarians in the tenth century as "fire worshippers". Since the Christian Church succeeded in suppressing the most spectacular and prominent customs like this one, the simple beliefs and habits surrounding the fireplace at home are all that remain of the former fire worship of the Hungarian people.

The first valid reference to the lighting of St. John's Fire was made in the sixteenth century. Miklós Telegdi, a Catholic preacher, referred to St. John's Fire in 1577 as a commemorative festival that the Church highly approved of. Two centuries later the ecclesiastical historian Inchofer noted that John the Baptist's festival had been adopted by the Hungarians in the eleventh century, but that the dazzling flames, the lighting of the fire, and the jumping and dancing had changed it into pagan superstition.

The fact that Hungarians throughout the country called the fire burning custom St. Ivan's fire, using the Slav name, while they called the saint himself St. John, is very interesting to note.

The saying "It's as long as St. Ivan's song" also dates from the sixteenth century. Gáspár Heltai wrote the following words in 1570: "I have heard that St. Ivan's song is so very long that if the devil began singing it, he would choke before he reached the end."

A collection of Hungarian proverbs from the nineteenth century refers this saying to a very beautiful series of songs that were performed during the fire-lighting festivals by Hungarians from the region of Nyitra. Like the Whitsun tradition this custom is also rich in mythical elements.

Many popular beliefs were linked to the lighting of St. John's Fire. According to Peter Bod's account in the 1750's, children used to scatter smutballs among the cabbages so that the caterpillars would not eat them, or in the fields of young corn to prevent the wheat from getting diseased. During the actual dancing round St. John's fire fruit was thrown into the flames, for it was believed that the fruit gained healing powers in this way. The children received these apples to prevent their falling ill. In Baranya County it was customary to leave some apples on the graves in the cemeteries too. Wreaths of wild flowers and grass were made on this day and hung on the front of the houses as protection against fire.

Harvest celebrations

Harvest festivals were held on the large estates where groups of peasants worked together or where special harvesters were hired to reap the crops. When the crops had all been gathered in, harvest wreaths or "corn babies" were made and presented ceremoniously to the landowner or farmer. The harvest was followed by supper and dancing. No festivals were held after harvests carried out by individual families. In Hungary, just as in other European countries, many popular beliefs and magic rituals were linked to the harvest, and particularly to the cutting of the last handful of corn in the field.

The "corn babies" at harvest time

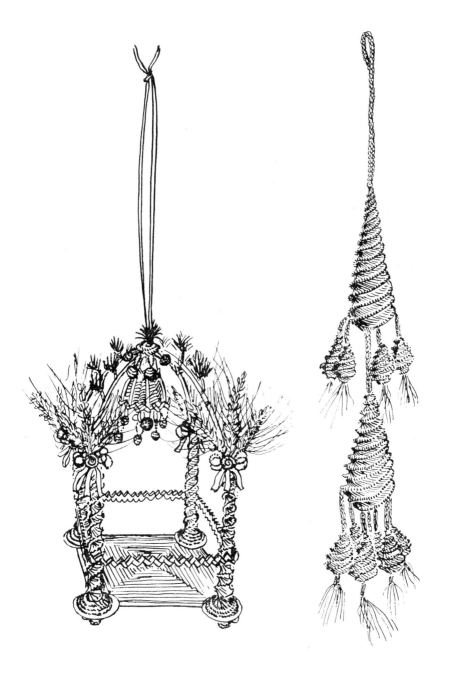

Autumnal festivities

The closing festivities of the agricultural year were held from September to November. It was during this period that the servants were paid for the year's work and the various herdsmen's festivals took place.

September 29th (St. Michael's Day) was the day for paying wages and for the herdsmen's reception. Farewell ceremonies were arranged by the herdsmen and especially the shepherds in East Hungary on October 26th (Demetrius' Day). This was also the day when the shepherds had to settle their accounts. Herdsmen's festivals were held in several parts of Transdanubia on Wendelin's Day—October 20th.

November 1st and 11th (St. Martin's Day) were also significant dates in the agricultural year. St. Martin's Day already figured in a fourteenth-century chronicle as an important occasion. In many regions of the country St. Martin's Day marked the end of the agricultural year and the grazing season. It was also the final day of the employment of agricultural labourers. It was customary in some western counties for the herdsmen to visit houses in a procession carrying "St. Martin's Whip" and reciting words of salutation.

The grape harvest festival was one of the highlights of the autumn *(Plates 25, 26 and XV)*. The vintners living in the Óbuda region of Budapest, who were mostly of German origin, used to hold very spectacular wine festivals up until a few years ago. The grape harvest ceremonies throughout the country included parades on horseback. Halls and bowers were decorated with bunches of grapes and anyone caught stealing any was punished. The grape harvest was followed by dancing.

On All Souls' Day graves were attended to and candles lit in the cemeteries. The houses in Catholic villages were also illuminated by candlelight, each candle burning in memory of someone who had died. In one or two places (for instance the village of Almamellék), food and drink were placed on the table for the dead.

A folk tradition known as the "girl market" used to be held in Baranya County during the autumn. Up until the Second World War it was performed regularly in the village of Görcsöny on November 5th. Mothers used to accompany their unmarried daughters to the "market", carrying all their best clothes. The girls put on different frocks several times during the day. This procedure was often repeated as many as five times. The girl market

XI. Carrying the bridal bed. Kazár, Nógrád County, 1970 ▶

was an opportunity for the young people to get to know one another. Mrs. György Gál's account of the custom is as follows:

"The boys lined up on both sides of the road while the unmarried girls walked up and down arm in arm. All the unmarried girls in the village had **49** to take part, and the young men used to stand and watch them. If a boy took a fancy to a particular girl, he would ask his acquaintances about her. At the end of the day the young people went to the inn, where the boys danced with the girls they had chosen. If a boy was content with a girl, he was introduced to her parents. There were occasions when this acquaintanceship ended in marriage."

Women's festivities in winter

When all the agricultural work was over, the women spent most of their working hours spinning. This occupation began in the second part of November and was often carried on until carnival season. Spinning was forbidden, however, during religious and popular festivities—for example, on St. Barbara's Day, St. Lucy's Day or at Christmas time.

The women and girls gathered together in the spinning-house and chatted, sang and joked as they worked. The church and secular authorities both agreed that the atmosphere in the spinning-house was highly immoral. The spinning "camp" was most certainly the largest centre where people gathered together and recited popular poetry and sang folk songs. In the written constitutions dating from the 1650's concerning the villages of Csík, Gyergyó and Kászonszék the following remarks can be read: "Although a law was passed forbidding meetings at night, there are some who have made light of this. The young men who idle the night hours away at the public house and the girls who visit the spinning-rooms and converse with young men must be stopped." *(Plate IV)*

Spinning-houses can only be found in one or two places today. In the 1950's, however, when spinning by hand was discontinued, some girls in Tura rented a room where they could sew and embroider together. A significant part of Hungarian lyrical poetry is linked to the spinning-house, which was also a natural "stage" for masquerading and mummery.

There were many days during November and December when popular custom forbade the woman to work. On such days the unmarried girls used

◄ XII. Carrying the bridal bed. Magyarvista (Viştea, Rumania), 1973

to try to guess who their husbands would be. In Somogy County St. Andrew's Day (November 30th) was the girls' fast-day; they were allowed only three grains of wheat and three drops of water to eat and drink, and then

they were supposed to dream about their future husbands. Slips of paper with boys' names on them were hidden in plum dumplings, and the first one that rose to the surface of the boiling water bore the name of the girl's husband to be.

Similar predictive customs were carried out on St. Catherine's Day (November 25th), St. Barbara's Day (December 4th), and St. Lucy's Day (December 13th).

The most significant women's customs during the month of December belonged to St. Lucy's Day. It was forbidden for women and girls to work, and there are many tales relating how St. Lucy punished those who dared to spin, weave, sew or wash on her day.

St. Lucy is said to fling away the spindle, and change the thread into tow, as punishment if she catches a woman spinning. Similar stories are told in connection with St. Barbara's Day when work was also forbidden.

"We don't usually work at all on St. Lucy's Day," a villager explained, "but once a woman was caught at it, and Lucy appeared before her and asked her why she was working. Didn't she know it was St. Lucy's Day? Whereupon the woman replied that by the time Lucy arrived she would have finished her weaving. But Lucy was there long before she had finished,

St. Lucy's stool

so she was unable to complete it. There was about a metre of weaving left to do but she couldn't finish." *(Harkányfürdő.)*

Masks are often worn on St. Lucy's Day. The women usually dress up in white and put thin white cloth over their faces. In this disguise they go round the village inspecting the children and reprimanding the lazy ones. In Horvátkimle the women dress in white on St. Lucy's Day and St. Barbara's Day too *(Plates 2 and 3)*.

The making of the special Lucy stool begins on St. Lucy's Day. According to popular belief the stool makes it possible for the person who made it to see the witches during Christmas Mass. There is hardly a village in the country where the superstitious tales about the Lucy stool are not known. We are told that the person making the stool must do a little work on it each day so that it is completed by Christmas Eve. He must then go to midnight Mass where he will be able to recognize the village witches by the horns on their heads. He must run home as fast as possible after mass, otherwise the witches will kill him. The story winds up by claiming that the surest way for the hero to escape the witches' revenge is to scatter poppy seeds along the road as he goes, for then the witches will be compelled to stop and pick them up.

In the western part of Hungary, particularly in South Transdanubia, small boys go round in the early morning on St. Lucy's Day and recite special texts. They carry hay or a piece of wood (which is better if it has been scrounged from somewhere) along with them and kneel down upon it to say their verse *(Plate 1)*. When they have finished the boys are sprinkled with corn or water by the inhabitants of the house. They "cast a spell" on the hens with the hay or a piece of wood so that the hens should lay many eggs all through the year. At the end of this procedure the children receive small gifts.

In Újkér the saying goes like this:

Lucy, Lucy click, cluck.
May your hens and geese be fine roosters!
May your axe and drills as strong and steady be,
As the roots of the gnarled oak tree!
May you have as many eggs as there are stars in the sky!
May you have as much money as there are husks in the barn!

May you slaughter a pig as big as the village bull!
And make a sausage as long as our main street!
May your ham be as thick as the widest cross-beam!

And may you have as much lard as there's water in the well!

St. Lucy's festival, like St. George's Day in spring, was also thought to be an occasion when the witches were free to play their evil tricks. There were two beliefs concerning Lucy—one that she was a saint and that December 13th was her feast day, and the other that she was a strange, demonic being. Before the calendar reforms, winter solstice fell on this day, making it the longest night and shortest day in the year. The name Lucy is actually related to light (lux).

Pig killing day

One of the greatest pleasures of the winter season is the pork feast, with its characteristic mummery and songs. The ethnologist István Tálasi in his book on the popular animal husbandry of Kiskunság (a region in Central Hungary) referred to the habit of chanting during the pig killing festival. "Some time ago in the village of Félegyháza," he writes, "it was the custom to chant on the evening of the pork feast. During the supper a group of young men or children began to chant rhythmical, rhyming verses beneath the window... The master invited them in and they then proceeded to recite a farewell verse to the pig, which embodied the whole process of preparation. The chanters were given some wine and a few crumbs before leaving." Mummery performed during the pig killing festival is a common sight on the Great Hungarian Plain. People, particularly young men, who would otherwise not take part in the feast, win admittance by disguising themselves and playing in the mummery, or by reciting amusing verses. The host and hostess do not regard the uninvited guests as intruders, they would in fact feel offended if the jokes and funny verses were not performed.

Greetings and jokes during the pork feast in Somogy County were sent on roughly made skewers. This was particularly popular in the villages of Zelicség, where it is still performed today. The custom is also practised in Almamellék, a village in Baranya County. During the pork feast the children, who have gathered outside one particular house, make a rattling noise and then poke a branch with spiky twigs through the door or the window. The best branch for the children is the one that has the most twigs on it. A letter, which contains practical jokes and crude messages, is fixed on to the upper prong. As the children are usually relatives or the children of neighbours, the host and hostess jokingly open the letter and laugh over its unprintable contents. Then they thread the many twigs of the "skewer" with different kinds of pork sausage and savoury scones, and put it back on the window sill, making sure that there are no dogs and cats around. The children emerge from their hiding places and take the laden "skewer" away, sharing the delicious contents among themselves.

St. Nicholas Day

The mummery on St. Nicholas Day and the giving of presents to children is not an old custom, as it was introduced into our country at the same time as the Christmas tree. There are, however, one or two documents from an earlier period that refer to the mummery on St. Nicholas Day, but they all come from West Hungary, where the custom was of Austrian origin. An interdict from the village of Csepreg in the year 1785 mentions this custom. "It is a known fact that since ancient times inhabitants from the village have appeared on the night before St. Nicholas the Bishop's Day, dressed in various garments and masks, and have been seen to wander from one house to another frightening innocent children with their perverse and scandalous appearance. It must be strongly emphasized that from now on no one is to dare to permit their families to appear in such gaudy clothes on the eve of St. Nicholas Day."

In the villages of West Transdanubia the children usually wear paper masks and sheepskin coats turned inside out; in their hands they carry chains, which they rattle *(Plates 4 and 5)*. In the village of Forró, near the town of Miskolc (Borsod-Abaúj-Zemplén County), the children wear wooden masks.

In the Ipoly river region a different type of mummery was practised. Here the boys used to read out amusing, mischievous texts while they acted as confessors to the "penitent" girls.

CUSTOMS CONNECTED WITH THE STAGES IN MAN'S LIFE

54   Just as festive customs are linked to the seasonal stages in the year, so the main stages in man's life are highlighted by festive customs. Ferenc Hont, the well-known Hungarian theatre expert, called the ritual succession of important events in peasant life "the theatre of life". In a profound study on the structure of these customs, van Gennep emphasized the transitional nature of the rituals and called them "rites of passage". He observed that the transition from one stage in life to another was carried out according to a definite ceremonial pattern that consisted of three main stages: the first stage, which involved the departure from the old status, a second transitional stage, when the individual fluctuated between the two stages, and the third and final stage, which signified the acceptance of the new status. These stages can be discerned in the funeral and wedding traditions and during the coming-of-age ceremony.

The theatre of life, in its entirety, came into being as a result of the dramatization of these transitional rites. The dramatic character of European wedding customs has often been cited as an appropriate example. Every participant has a special part to play during the wedding ceremony, and individual feelings and inclinations can only be expressed in relation to this particular role. The bride, for example, should show sorrow at leaving her parents, and joy when she steps into her future home. She ought not eat or drink a lot and so on.

Traditional funeral rites are carried out in a similar way. The custom of singing a dirge is a traditional procedure, which allows individual emotion to be expressed within the traditional framework provided by the community, and at the same time makes it possible for real feelings to be concealed.

As we have seen so far folk customs provided the community with predetermined roles that not only helped them over the difficult transitions in life, but also forced them to participate. These roles in life are observed so often from childhood onwards that their acquisition takes place almost unconsciously. The older members of the community do, however, consciously teach the practice of these traditional roles. Hungarian experts in folk music have observed how old women have taught their grandchildren the traditional method of keening, so that there should be no doubt in their minds of the correct way when the time comes for them to take part. In the village of Galgamácsa children play "weddings" at Easter and other times, following all the traditional conventions, in a sort of rehearsal for the great part they must later play. Special organizing and functionary roles are played by the best men at the weddings, for it is their responsibility to see that everything takes place in the right order.

Great significance was attached to the practice of magic in the customs linked to the stages in a man's life. Superstitious rituals were performed particularly at birth and death—the two dangerous periods in life—in an effort to protect the individual concerned.

Birth, christening

Ritual actions surrounded the newborn baby from the first moment of its life. These rites were determined by several factors—by traditional medicine based on popular experience, by social customs, which included the reception, as it were, of the baby into the family and community, and many procedures of a purely superstitious nature that were believed to protect the helpless baby from harmful, supernatural powers.

No other branch of village life has changed as radically in the last few decades as the customs surrounding the newborn child. The younger generation no longer believes in the old superstitions, and thanks to good medical care and the painstaking work of doctors, infant mortality in the villages has decreased to a minimum. The customs described in the following paragraphs are all things of the past.

According to the procedure that was once part of the custom of receiving a baby into the family's community, the baby was put on the ground, then picked up by the father, who placed his hat on the baby's head for a second, or if the child was a boy, he was sat on the horse in the stable.

It was believed that certain signs pointed to the child's future, its latent talent and skill. Predictions were also made according to the time of year when the baby was born. The Csángós of Moldavia shared the South-East European belief that the newborn baby was visited by three demoniac women who determined its future. This superstition was not known to other Hungarian ethnic groups, but there was a widespread legend, according to which a voice occasionally predicted that a child would drown in later life. And there was nothing that the family could do to avoid this, for the prophecy would come true. In many stories the child was found dead on the spiky branches covering the well.

The midwives who assisted at birth were thought to possess extraordinary powers. Although this was a common belief, it was particularly strong in Sárrét where every midwife was reputed to have magic skill and people were careful not to offend them in any way for fear of harming the child. The superstitions surrounding the midwife obviously sprang from the fact that she assisted in one of the most important events in life, an event that from the man's point of view was shrouded in mystery. It was the men, therefore, who regarded the midwife as someone who had dealings with the supernatural.

In 1964 several superstitious tales about midwives and their magic power were collected from Sárrétudvari and the neighbouring countryside. The midwife appeared in one of the stories as a ghost in a white robe. The old documents from witchcraft trials often accused midwives of sorcery.

Folk customs stipulated exactly how many days the mother must stay in bed. If she did get up for some reason or other, she placed a broom in the bed to ward off evil spirits from the little one. Not only the "bad spirits" were feared to be dangerous, for it was also believed that even well-meaning visitors could cause harm and "take away the mother's milk or make the baby ill."

The newborn baby and the young mother were also protected by the so-called "Virgin Mary's Bed", in which they both lay for the first few weeks. The bed was curtained off with a sheet or mosquito net, and all sorts of objects believed to have magic power were placed beside the mother. The mother and child were not disturbed here by the activity of the family. Great significance was attributed to the first bath; money, herbs and various objects were put in the water as they determined the good characteristics of the child.

"Godmother dishes" containing soup, stuffed cabbage and some sweets were brought to the mother during confinement to save her from having to cook and speed her complete recovery. The custom in Jászfelsőszentgyörgy was that the godmother had to bring omelette, soup, doughnuts and fried chicken in such quantity that she could not use her hands and had to open the door with her elbow.

XIII. The wedding party. Méra (Mera, Rumania), 1971 ▶

If a baby in a Catholic family was disabled in some way the midwife immediately performed a "dry christening". The decrees of sixteenth-century Protestant synods all alluded to this action, without exception, and strictly prohibited the midwife from christening a baby even if it was dan- **57** gerously ill.

People were afraid that if a baby was not christened, it would be hurt or would suffer from the "evil eye". Nicknames, like Little Ugly One were given to the baby before the christening, for it was believed that this misled the evil spirits. According to popular belief a child fell ill because it had been exchanged for another by evil spirits. Many folk sayings gave advice on how the child could be changed back again. The procedure suggested in these sayings was generally that the changeling lying in swaddling-clothes must somehow be made to talk and betray himself. One method, for example, was to give the baby some milk in a small earthenware pot with a large spoon, and watch to see what it would do. As the "changed" child did not know how to eat, it would begin to cry out in vexation. This action would compel the evil spirits to return the true child.

Baptism was a grand festive occasion for a very long time, sometimes almost equalling the wedding in its splendour. A decree at the synod in Debrecen in 1567 forbade and fined young women for taking part in the celebrations following the birth of a child that went on late into the night. Different factors were taken into consideration when choosing godparents in the various ethnic groups. Godparents generally played important roles in the child's life, and the godfather was often appointed best man at the wedding.

Wedding

The second major "transitional ritual" in man's life—the initiation ceremony—has already been mentioned in the passage describing the customs on Innocents' Day. Hungarian ethnographers and sociographers have often described the pattern of life for a boy and girl in traditional Hungarian peasant culture. In general the girls were kindly treated and their mothers always tried to give them a few happy years with no responsibilities before their marriage. If the family were fairly well off they did their utmost to dress the daughter in beautiful clothes. We have already mentioned some of the

◄ *XIV. Boys obstructing the bride's path with a rope. Szék (Sic, Rumania), 1974*

The emblem used at the initiation ceremony

annual courting customs, like the erection of the maypole for the unmarried girls, the wassailing songs young men sang to them, the custom of sprinkling water at Easter and the visit paid to them on Innocents' Day.

Carefree life came to an end when the wedding ceremony was over. **59**

There are documents that describe wedding festivities at the time of the settlement of the Magyars in Hungary in the last years of the ninth century and in the following centuries. Gardízi, a Persian historian, writing about the Hungarian wedding ceremony in the years 1050–1052, made the following observation: "During the marriage proposal ceremony the custom is that the young man offers a price for the girl, usually in the form of animals, which depends on the financial status of the bride. When they decide on a suitable price the girl's father takes the boy's father into his house and collects all the furs he has—sable, ermine, squirrel, beechmorten, and the fur from the stomach of the fox; and these together with brocade material and skins, enough for ten leather coats, are all rolled up in a carpet and tied on to the horse belonging to the boy's father, who is then sent home. Once at home he collects and sends all the things that have been decided on to complete the exchange, usually money, animals and other chattels, to the girl's father. The girl is then taken home."

Vestiges of Hungarian antiquity, including the old wedding customs, have been preserved in the language to this day. The word *eladó lány*, for example, meaning 'girl to be married off or sold', was used when referring to unmarried girls; the word *vő* for 'son-in-law' originates from the word *vevő* meaning 'bidder'; *meny*, the word for 'daughter-in-law', originally referred to the fur (*menyét* = weasel) that was given in exchange for the daughter, and so on.

Traces of the leviratical custom also live on in rustic speech, because a woman still calls her husband's younger brother 'my younger husband', and the older brother 'my older husband'. According to the custom followed by the Magyars at the time of their settlement in Hungary, the husband's brother had the right to claim his wife if he died; moreover, our archaeologists and historians claim that a boy had the right to marry his own stepmother. The explanation for this is that if a widow remarried outside the family, they had to pay back her "purchase price", so it was obviously in their interests to keep her in the family.

Medieval chronicles describe other features connected with the marriage ceremony in this country. An ancient Hungarian legend has survived in Simon Kézai's *Chronicle* written in the thirteenth century. It tells of Hunor and Magor and their followers, who were guided by a hind, and how they snatched the womenfolk of the sons of Belár and married them. Among the women were the two daughters of the Alan prince. Hunor and Magor married them and their descendants became the Huns and the Magyars.

Two conclusions have been drawn from this legend. One is that the heathen Hungarian marriage customs were exogamous. This seems quite probable as the Ob-Ugrians, the nearest akin in language, still kept rigidly to the rules of exogamy until a few decades ago. Marriage within their own clan was impossible for the Ob-Ugrians.

Over the centuries, however, exogamy in the customs of Hungary pretty well disappeared. By the eighteenth and nineteenth centuries the general custom was that a boy married a girl from his own village, in fact sometimes she had to be someone from his side of the village as it was considered improper if he married a girl living at the other end. This was obviously linked with the unwillingness to divide up the small plots of land. But it cannot be considered a compulsory rule. The question of religion was also very important when considering marriage. Marriage used to take place, for example, between the inhabitants of the Protestant villages in the district of Sárköz and the Protestant villages in Baranya County.

The second conclusion drawn from the legend mentioned above is that the conquering Hungarian tribes procured their wives by abduction. The abduction of women certainly did occur among the Hungarians, just as it did among other peoples, because it meant that they did not pay anything for the girl (the legend of the rape of the Sabine women immediately comes to mind). Gardízi's above-quoted description, on the other hand, proves that marriage was usually based on the exchange of gifts, and that the abduction of girls was an exception and not the general practice. Statute-books from the Middle Ages and later show that the carrying off of women did occur in certain cases. If a young couple wanted to marry without the consent of their parents, the boy would "steal" the girl, for in this case the law insured the possibility of an agreement at a later date. The mock "stealing of women" still took place between the two World Wars when families were unable to produce the exorbitant sums of money necessary for the wedding feast. In such cases the young couple would leave the neighbourhood with the knowledge of their parents and then return after a time when a splendid wedding would be considered most unbefitting.

Some Hungarian medieval chronicles contain descriptions of the ancient wedding ceremony. An account of the nuptials of Zolta, the son of Árpád, who was leader of the Magyar tribe, can be found in the chronicle *Gesta Hungarorum* which has survived in a MS dating from the thirteenth century. The following is an extract: "Chief Árpád and all his leaders arranged a splendid feast during the wedding festivites and from day to day following the nuptial custom he joined his knights, who came from all corners of the country, in great merry-making. The young ones played games in front of the chief and his noblemen."

It can definitely be said that compared to other Hungarian folk customs, those connected with the wedding have retained the most of their structure. For today marriage festivites are still composed of two parts, namely the legal agreement between the two families (which was later sanctified by the State and Church) and the spectacularly planned ritual that contains artistic motifs of great significance. Experts on popular unwritten law are correct when they state that the wedding consisted of two main legal actions: the engagement and the giving away of the daughter. According to legal customs engagement (consisting of the actual betrothal ceremony and the exchange of engagement presents) was compulsory for both parties. The innumerable village rituals that still surround the giving away ceremony today show that this is the time when the actual "contract" is fulfilled.

At the turn of the century village wedding rites in Hungary showed some regional differences, although a common structure could be distinguished in the background. In the villages couples were generally matched for purely economic reasons, so that young people seldom had a say in the matter as to who their future husband or wife would be. Before proposing marriage it was customary for the boy's family to send relatives or acquaintances to the house where the girl lived to find out whether her family would be pleased to see them. If the person sent to intercede in this way was an old woman she might be given a present. Often she was teased and called names because of her task. If the message brought back was favourable the young man visited the girl's house accompanied by relatives or his best man. After a successful marriage proposal the boy's parents also paid a visit to the house.

Years ago a "dowry letter" was written before the engagement took place, in which the future husband promised his wife money, land or other chattels as an insurance in case he should die first.

The marriage proposal was followed by the engagement, when the bride-to-be gave her fiancé a small token, usually a scarf or shirt, and received an article of clothing or some money in return. This exhange of tokens was regarded as a sort of deposit on the future marriage. If one of them broke off the engagement for no apparent reason, the token had to be returned. Long ago the engagement was attended by two best men, who acted as the legal witnesses of the ceremony. The position of the best man is now only considered an honour as all former legal responsibilities have disappeared.

Engagement ended in marriage in church or at a registry office and was then followed by the village wedding feast, which is still performed today in all its splendour and gaiety *(Plates 29, 30, XII–XIV)*. Expensive weddings were forbidden by the authorities for centuries. In the eighteenth century Sámuel Tessedik wrote the following: "I knew a village farmer who lived quite comfortably ten years ago and was never struck by any sort of catastrophe. He was not a squanderer, but he fell a victim of his own habit of throwing huge wedding feasts, so much so that in his old age he avoided the humiliation of begging by stealing bread."

The wedding feast is preceded by the bride's lament and farewell. True emotion was often expressed in these laments, for it meant that the girl would have to leave the shelter of her parents' home and that from then on she must carry out the orders of her parents-in-law. In those cases where the choice of a husband had been made for material reasons rather than any feeling of mutual attraction, the lament was particularly sincere and full of apprehension. One of the most beautiful farewell songs is the one Zoltán Kodály found in 1909 in the village of Menyhe, Nyitra County (Mechenice, Czechoslovakia):

> *As a shoot of marjoram by the wayside growing,*
> *Likes not its humble home and hides itself away,*
> *From sunlight and moonlight taking a sad farewell,*
> *So Ágnes, to father and mother, mother and father,*
> *To girlfriends, to girlfriends and those who support you,*
> *Farewell, my dear Ágnes, you must now say farewell!*

One of the customs included in the wedding rites was the ceremonial transportation of the bride's bed linen—sheets, pillows and an eiderdown—to her new home *(Plate XI)*. Nowadays, however, the village brides usually take furniture and other equipment, like a washing machine and a television set, with them.

Before the marriage ceremony could be performed the giving away of the daughter had to take place. As this was the point when the bride was actually handed over, the custom culminated in a complexity of innumerable rituals. Occasionally the suitors were only allowed into the bride's house if they were able to answer the riddles put to them. The following account was heard in the village of Sárrétudvari: "The groomsman arrived at the house and he shouted, 'Well, this young man 'ere has come for his bride-to-be, who lives within.' 'Which road did you take to get here?' asked the bride's father. 'Which road? Why, the main road!' one of them answered. 'Now, there you see. I told you there's no maiden here! That road doesn't lead this way!' If there was someone among them who knew the answer—road to love—the door was immediately opened and they were let in."

One very popular joke played on the suitors in most regions of the country was to change the bride. A veiled old woman was brought in, or a goat, or one of the bridesmaids, and of course the suitors refused every one of them. It was only after performing these planned scenes that the real bride was brought forth.

The giving away ceremony was followed by the reception into the new family. In Jászság, for example, on entering her new home the bride would rub the stove three times. In other districts a shovel, broom and bucket were thrown in front of the bride as she stepped from the cart. If she did not pick them up they would exclaim, "Oh dear! This girl will be lazy!" In Gyöngyöspata and Somogy County the custom was to place a bucket of water in front of the bride. She had to kick it over as this would ensure "easy birth" for her children.

The number of wedding meals depended on how long the festivities lasted. A few decades ago weddings of three or more days were not uncommon. The cooking and preparation of the various dishes followed in strict order. On the Hungarian Plain the making of special noodles for the soup formed a separate ritual in itself and was accompanied by dancing.

If a girl married someone from another village or moved after the wedding to another part of her village, the boys from her neighbourhood used to put various obstacles along the road that the cart would take; they would build a fire, for example, or tie thick pieces of straw rope across the road *(Plate XIV)*. The groomsman was responsible for clearing away the obstacles and making sure that the bride arrived safely in her new home. It was also the groomsman's duty to invite the guests, to entertain and serve them; he was in fact the very soul of the wedding feast.

64

Today the wedding dinner is followed by the custom of tying the bride's hair up, an indication that she is accepted as a married woman. For many centuries the ritual of removing the girl's headdress and donning the cap has been the symbol of reaching womanhood.

One of the striking features of the Hungarian wedding dinner is the custom of reciting special verses as each course is being served. Countless collections of "groomsmen's verses" were printed during the last century. These poems were handed down to later generations and many regional versions began to appear. The soup, stuffed cabbage, roast meat, gruel and wine are all accompanied by their own particular verses. The meat casserole, for example, might be followed by this rhyme:

Dear wedding guests, I make my toast,
The tale to tell of this fine roast,
I pray you, do not think I boast.
For 'twas indeed a trial of strength,
I fought that bull for seven days length.
The brute once got me underneath,
As we were struggling on the heath,
And I escaped by the skin of my teeth.
So ends my toast, but now the sequel,
A feast that never had its equal.

(From the Jászság region)

Another tradition known throughout the country was the collection of "gruel money", when the cooks appeared during the supper with their hands bandaged, complaining bitterly that the gruel had scolded them. The guests then put money on the wooden spoons held out by the cooks, and this rep-

resented the "cost of the saucepan or 'the gruel' ". Another tradition at weddings was that the young people who were not related to either family were allowed to join in the feast at a given time, when they could eat and drink and take part in the dancing. In Transdanubia the bridegroom's best friends used to arrive at the appointed time and entertain the wedding guests. They were called the "three dancers" in Győr-Sopron County. Uninvited guests at weddings on the Great Hungarian Plain used to wear masks.

65

A wedding mask. Somogy County

Zsigmond Móricz, the novelist, described this custom in a short story entitled *The Butterfly* that was published in 1925. One of the characters is Zsuzsika, a girl who arrives at her unfaithful lover's wedding in Debrecen dressed up as a boy. "There is an ancient custom in Debrecen," writes Zsigmond Móricz, "according to which young people and children, even those who were not invited, frequent weddings wearing masks, chase after the bride's cart, and stand staring in at the door of the house where the wedding is being celebrated, in the hope that they will get a glass or two of wine and a leg of chicken." But to return to the story, Zsuzsika, disguised in a broad-brimmed hat and a man's coat hovers about until she finally manages to catch the attention of Jóska, the young husband. He suddenly makes a decisive move and, leaving his newly wedded bride, disappears into the crowd with Zsuzsika. From a distance Jóska calls back to his mother-in-law, "Please forgive me, but I shall never go to the farm! I am poor and I must live with a poor girl! God be with you!"

Dramatic scenes and dances were performed during the wedding celebrations. The "burial game", a parody of the funeral, was often played, and in Baranya County this took the form of the farewell ritual to the grey horse. In Göcsej Death himself appeared and warned the wedding guests in a long poem that their gay spirits were all in vain, for the time would come when they would be struck down too.

◀ *XVI. Heaven's bridegroom. Bridesmaids escort the deceased young man on his last journey. Rimóc, Nógrád County, 1970*

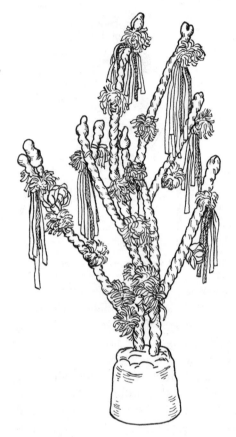

The tree of life at a wedding

More magic rites were practised in the dawn following the wedding feast. In South Transdanubia the bride used to draw water from the well and symbolically wash the guests. Brides from the Palots region had to jump over a fire, a ritual first mentioned in the sixteenth century.

The "tree of life" was an interesting feature of the village wedding. A branch was covered with pastry and sometimes decorated with pastry figures of boys and girls. The branch was called "furry one" in the villages beside Kis-Küküllő, but elsewhere it was known as the green branch or tree of life. Other sweets and cakes were also made on the occasion of the wedding. "Kulcsos kalinkó"—milk bread rolls—were thrown at the guests arriving at weddings in Győr-Sopron County. It is customary in Orosháza to bake plaited loaves and decorate them with birds and flowers.

There is an immense range of popular poetry connecting to the wedding. Apart from the verses accompanying the feast that have already been mentioned, the bride's farewell songs, best man's poems, love songs and various wedding games were all very well known in Hungary. In the one or two places where peasant costume is still worn, the village wedding is a really attractive and impressive sight *(Plates 28–30)*.

Funeral

Funeral rituals were generally more conservative than other customs and contained very ancient beliefs. The Church inflicted very severe punishment **67** on those who buried their dead according to pagan beliefs. This resulted in the gradual disappearance of pagan burial rites, particularly the more spectacular customs. The heathen superstitions connected with the dead, however, strongly resisted the laws of the Church.

It is possible that the Hungarian Conquerors, like their Finno-Ugrian relatives, also believed that a person possessed several souls and that after death one of them departed. An important task of old Hungarian shamans was probably to lead one of the dead person's souls to a new dwelling place. No trace of this ancient practice can be found among popular customs today, but we can determine the nature of this belief in the plurality of souls from certain linguistic forms.

A characteristic phenomenon of the burial places of Hungarian noblemen, before the country was converted to Christianity, was the presence of bones from horses and horse gear. These objects were found in the graves of men and women alike, in fact the trappings in the women's graves were usually even more ornamental. In general the heathen Magyars did not bury the whole horse with the dead, but only the head and legs, whereas whole skeletons have been discovered in Avar graves. The following objects were unearthed in a single woman's grave in Csorna, Győr-Sopron County: horse's bones, trappings ornamented with rosettes, stirrups, a bridle, buckle, knife, some earrings, and a silver ring. Women's graves, containing trappings decorated with rosettes have always been found amongst other similar Hungarian graves dating from the Conquest. Single rich men's graves have also come to light. One was found in Geszteréd (Szabolcs-Szatmár County), for example, in which a large collection of sabres, purse plates decorated with a palmette design, silver ornaments for belts, stirrups, a bridle and other objects were uncovered.

Another kind of grave for single men has been found, which contained the skull and leg bones of a horse, together with simple weapons and utensils.

A completely different type of burial-ground has been excavated, also dating from the Conquest of Hungary, which is considered to be an extended family grave. The richest grave, situated roughly in the middle, is where the head of the family was buried. The men and boys were buried to the left of the central grave, the women to the right.

68   Family burial-grounds with a different layout have also come to light. There is one in the town of Kolozsvár (Napoca, Rumania), for example, where the graves form three lines. The first row is composed of the graves of horsemen, while men, women and children are buried in the other two rows. Sabres can always be found among the weapons in the family graves of this type, but never double-edged swords.

Other graves, also dating from the Conquest and containing the remains of noblemen and well-to-do Hungarians, contrast sharply with the above type, since among the accessories of the man's grave the double-edged, straight sword is characteristic and there are no horse's bones or trappings in the women's graves.

Specialists were faced with a much greater task when trying to differentiate between the graves of common Hungarians and those of other peoples living in Hungary, as far less accessories were put into these graves. Swords and sabres have been found in horsemen's graves where the studded belts, which archaeologists consider to have been a sign of rank and dignity, are missing. Other men's graves have been unearthed containing bows and arrow-heads. Hungarian archaeologists compare the burial rites of the heathen Magyars to those of the Avars, Sarmatians and Scythians.

The dead person's face, in graves dating from the Conquest, is generally turned towards the rising sun. In 1958 a grave was found in Szabolcs County by archaeologists containing a skull that was covered with a piece of leather marked with small silver plates for the eyes and mouth. This finding caused a great sensation, for the custom of using death masks at funerals was practised until a few years ago by some Finno-Ugrian peoples.

The appearance of burial grounds underwent a radical change in the early Árpádian period. The bones of horses disappeared, for the "equestrian graves" were strictly forbidden by the Church. It appears that during the Middle Ages the horse, which would originally have been buried with its master, was presented to the Church instead or its price was paid; at least there seems to be a reference to this in a document written in 1383. Following a custom from the West, the remains of noblemen were placed in the crypts of churches, or in the closed yards surrounding them. Families, on the other hand, still liked to be buried together, despite the fact that this custom had been prohibited by law for many centuries. The synods warned followers to avoid the lamentations and superstitious splendour of funerals and to refrain from practising funeral feasts, prayers and the collection of alms for the dead. Decrees introduced by the Council of the Governor-General in the eighteenth century placed cemeteries outside the town and repeatedly forbade the expensive funeral feasts.

By the turn of the century there were many elements in Hungarian funeral customs that were similar to those of neighbouring countries. The approach of death was prophesied by the behaviour of animals. Pillows stuffed with hen's feathers were taken away from the dying person, because according to popular belief it was impossible for anyone to die if their heads were resting on pillows of this kind. A person who was dying often wished to be taken out of bed and placed on the ground as it was thought easier to die there. Mirrors and other objects with shiny surfaces were covered up when a person died. The window was opened so that the dead person's soul could depart with ease; the opposite also occurred in some regions where windows were kept closed if there was a dead person in the house. Fires were put out in the house and cooking had to be done at the neighbours. A vigil was kept at night in the house of the deceased, during which the members of the community sang and talked. The vigil was an important occasion for the recital of popular poetry.

The dead person was always carried out of the house feet first. In many regions the coffin was placed on a frame with four legs, called "St. Michael's Horse". Numerous magic rites were performed; small children, for example, were made to touch the toes of dead parents that they should forget them easier.

The news of someone's death was made known to the community by ringing the bells; the knoll differed according to whether the dead person was a man, woman or child. Burials were sometimes performed by voluntary societies known as "Calendar Societies". As far as we know these societies were first mentioned in Hungary in the eleventh century. Their name comes from the fact that on the first day of every month they gathered together to settle various matters. During the period in history when guilds were functioning, these groups made sure that suitable funerals were arranged for the members of each guild.

Before burial fastenings and buttons were left undone on the clothes of the dead person, and coins were placed on his eyes. One custom practised throughout the country was to place a sickle or some other sharp bladed

instrument on the dead person's stomach, so that "it should not swell." This rational explanation probably took the place of an older superstitious belief. In some instances when coffin measurements were being taken, branches and reeds were used to measure the length of the dead person. This custom was also practised by the Croatians living in Hungary, who placed the reed they had used on top of the grave after the funeral. The favourite personal belongings of the deceased were put into the grave, and sometimes an object that had been forgotten was included for someone who died before. In Jászság it was believed that the person who had died most recently kept guard over the gateway of the cemetery until he was relieved by the next one.

The wooden headboards erected on the graves in the cemeteries of East Hungary and Transylvania as well as in other Protestant districts of the country are particularly interesting. The most characteristic types are the headboards with halberds and the scaphoid and knob-shaped posts. The last two are considered to have human forms in some regions. The boat-shaped posts in the village cemeteries of Szamosszeg and Szatmárcseke, for example, certainly do give the impression of human figures, producing the weirdest effect on snowy, winter days, as if one was walking by a row of idols. This stylized human form could have been intended in the creation of the knob-shaped posts. Specialists think they have discovered a Turkish influence on these posts, but unfortunately they are all falling into rapid decay, and will probably disappear completely without our having ever solved the secret of their origin and meaning. This seems all the more probable as hardly any historical references exist.

The custom of holding a ceremonial wedding on the death of a young man or girl was still practised in most parts of the country at the turn of the century *(Plates 35 and XVI)*. The mourners used to dress in festive clothes on these occasions and walk in procession to the grave. The fiancé, lover or occasionally a relative, acted as "bride" or "bridegroom" to the deceased and were given presents by the family in reward for their pains. The deceased boy was accompanied by bridesmaids and the girl by best men.

Historical documents refer to mourning garments of various colours, namely red, yellow and white. The white mourning dress is still known in

Scaphoid grave posts

Wooden grave head board

Csököly and a few other villages in Somogy County *(Plates 32, 33 and 34)*. Some decades ago white mourning was still worn by the women in the region of Ormánság. Today village mourners have been influenced by town habits and dress generally in black.

The informal recital of laments is one of the most archaic and most beautiful poetic elements in Hungarian funeral customs. The lament has survived to this day despite the fact that the Church disapproved of the custom and always strove to replace it with religious songs and texts. In these laments relatives address their deceased, combining traditional forms with their own personal thoughts.

It is thanks to Hungarian folklorists that a large collection of laments has been brought to light in the last two decades, at a time when this poetic form was considered almost extinct.

The past history of these songs of lamentation fades into obscurity. According to medieval Latin chronicles they were practised in very early times, when it was also customary to sing dirges in first person singular at the burial rites of valiant chiefs and soldiers. On these occasions the wailer used to speak in the deceased's name and give an account of his deeds. (The memory of this custom has been preserved on some epitaphs, which are written in the name of the deceased and describe how he died and who he was.)

The loud wailing dirge was compulsory in a way, for people thought very badly of anyone who did not mourn over their relatives.

The following dirge was noted down in the village of Szerep (Hajdú-Bihar County) in 1964:

> *Mother, sweet mother,*
> *We have lost our dear mother.*
> *Pain and suffering she bore; we watched her and could not help.*
> *Dear God, you tried her sorely, bowed her down with sickness.*
> *Mother, dear mother, are you resting now?*
> *Come brothers and sisters, stand closely together,*
> *Let us mourn our dear mother,*
> *Let us sing a mournful song.*
> *Three score years and ten she lived.*
> *She was so good to us,*
> *She granted every wish.*

With loving care she brought us up.
Now they are taking her away;
Death has taken away our beloved mother.
Dear father, how lonely you must be.
Here we shall stay, we will not leave you.
Pray God, bless our sweet mother!
She shall sleep in the womb of the earth,
And her spirit shall rejoice in heavenly splendour.

Wooden grave posts

SOCIAL AND LEGAL CUSTOMS

Popular legal customs and social traditions spread to all those customs that did not come under the jurisdiction of the State and Church. These unwritten laws also determined the moral conduct of the community. The customs dealt first and foremost with marriages and the laws of succession, but also settled family relationships and the legal problems concerning illegitimate children.

Legal customs regulated the methods of buying and selling, which included the ancient habit of drinking toasts. The election of the mayor in the village, fire regulations and all the general, daily tasks of the community—like the upkeep of the communal pasture, the reception of herdsmen and the protection of vineyards and fields—were regulated by popular tradition. Legal customs also settled the order of communal work. The custom of whipping, which disappeared only a few years ago, was performed when boundaries were marked. A child was laid on the spot to be marked and "whipped" so that he should never forget the boundary mark.

Economic life and all areas of work, including the construction of houses, were surrounded by distinct customs. The memory of the ancient practice of offering a sacrifice when a building was completed still persists in some areas in a much simplified form, where eggs are mixed with the lime-mortar. Another custom I witnessed in Szerep (Hajdú-Bihar County) recently when a letter was placed in the foundations of a house under construction. It contained the owner's and builder's names, the date of construction and an exact list of all expenses.

Folk customs regulated the rights and obligations of each member of the family and their eating habits. The Palots people of the Mátra region lived for many centuries in large families where the oldest man was head of the family. He shared out the work every day and the entire wealth of the family was in his hands. The duty of every member was determined by customary law, for the joint effort of the family was essential to its survival and prosperity.

The question of succession was considered to be a legal custom of paramount importance. Years ago the custom was that the male side of the family inherited, the girls' inheritance being much smaller in value. The youngest son had the privilege to stay in his father's house.

The moral attitude of the people was also determined by popular custom.

Offenders of the accepted moral code were ridiculed and in some areas their sins were publicly announced, especially during festivals, like St. George's Day or carnival time.

Among the traditional methods of punishment in Hungary one spectacu- lar custom was practised in a few regions. This is actually the Hungarian version of a tradition known to many peoples of Europe under the name of mock serenade or charivari.

This custom was a lesson to those who violated the community's moral sense, and was directed against young couples, for example, who could not live together in peace, or anyone who was guilty of conjugal infidelity. The method of punishment was to bring the guilty person to shame by shouting out their sins.

In the villages of Biharugra and Körösnagyharsány the custom was directed primarily against couples who quarrelled and were then reconciled, and especially against women who left their husbands and returned later. But the humiliating "sounding of bells" was also performed if a couple were living together illegally. Despite the fact that people were afraid of this custom which caused such degradation (there was a case in Körösnagyharsány of a person who went blind in the disputes that followed the "sounding of bells"), young couples often separated temporarily, usually because the young wife could not get on with her mother-in-law. In most cases the brunt of the punishment was borne by the women, rather than the men, although the neighbours generally knew all the details of the argument and would shout them out during the mock serenade, so that both parties got what they deserved.

The mock serenade carried out by the village communities in Sárrét was a means by which the young wife was forced to adapt herself to her husband's family and learn to live in harmony with them. The custom itself took the form of a mock wedding. The "sounding of the bells" began on the evening of the day when it was believed the estranged couple had made it up and the young wife had returned to her husband. Following the pattern of a real wedding the three evenings were called the engagement, the making of noodles and the wedding. The main part was played by the "priest", who married the "new couple" with unmentionable verses. The priest was followed by all the young men from the village, who carried whips, mortars and bells, and made an infernal noise.

Couples always tried to avoid the unpleasant uproar, sometimes they would move temporarily to another place and hide away, or they would leave their native village for good. The family used to prepare in advance for the mock serenaders, and pour dirty water, for example, over the noisy crowd. Fighting was almost unavoidable in the clashes that ensued with the whole village taking part. The following account was given in Biharugra:

"The road was covered with mud when they chased the serenaders away. People fled in all directions, one leaving his hat behind, another his boot. They were ashamed to collect them the next morning; but if another serenade occurred they would have gone there too, because the custom was in their blood and they could not refuse to go."

Pál Szabó, a Hungarian novelist born in Biharugra, also described the custom in his novel *Őszi vetés* (The Sowing of Winter Corn):

"The young couple are standing in the porch in the midst of the scandalous riot clasped in each other's arms and crying like children... The noise explodes upon them like a wall caving in or a beam splitting across. But they must have known that this was a custom or rather rule that no one could evade."

SCIENTIFIC RESEARCH ON FOLK CUSTOMS IN HUNGARY

The first chapter of this book contains a short account of Sándor Réső Ensel's monograph. This was the first book to deal entirely with the description of folk customs, although it was by no means the first scholarly written essay on customs.

A great deal of information on Hungarian folk customs has been found in ecclesiastical works from the Middle Ages onwards, in sermons, synodical declarations, polemical treatises, etc. Foreigners in Hungary were often impressed by the Corpus Christi processions, the customs of the guilds and the mock funerals. Seventeenth-century memoirs, eighteenth-century state documents and old guide-books all contain references to folk customs. The first real ethnographic descriptions can be found in the scientific journals that began to appear at the beginning of the nineteenth century. Since the middle of the nineteenth century every treatise or book containing a description of one particular area, county, ethnic group or village is bound to include a regional description of the popular traditions. An enumeration of them all would fill a whole book.

Experts in the nineteenth century approached the subject from various angles. The magic rites and the beliefs connected to them aroused great interest; Arnold Ipolyi's *Magyar mythologia* [Hungarian Mythology] (1854) contains a detailed description of the seasonal festivals in Hungary.

Interest in the spectacular and dramatic rituals was also aroused very early and became linked, from the very beginning of ethnographic research, with the study of folk plays. The first volume of the "Anthology of Hungarian Folk Poetry" began with Pál Gyulai's description of the Nativity plays and it was here that he expounded his views on medieval Hungarian miracle plays. Accounts of popular traditions continued to appear in the later volumes of this series. Gyula Sebestyén devoted the fourth and fifth volumes entirely to the custom of wassailing *(Regös énekek* [Wassailing Songs] and *A regösök* [The Wassailers], 1902).

Henrik Wlislocki's monograph was published at the end of the last century in German *(Aus dem Volksleben der Magyaren)*. Almost all the prominent ethnographers and folklorists at the end of the last century and in the first decades of the twentieth century contributed to the collection or interpretation of folk customs; Lajos Kálmány, Lajos Katona, Béla Vikár, Ferenc Gönczi and János Berze Nagy immediately come to mind.

The analysis of many important customs appeared in the period between the two World Wars. Zsigmond Szendrey and Ákos Szendrey wrote studies on practically every Hungarian folk custom. A summary of their work can be found in the fourth volume of the handbook *A Magyarság Néprajza* [Hungarian Ethnography].

The chapter on dramatic traditions in the third volume of "Hungarian Ethnography" was written by Károly Viski. He also wrote a summary of Hungarian folk traditions which appeared in English and German.—Géza Róheim's book *Magyar néphit és népszokások* [Hungarian Popular Beliefs and Folk Traditions], published in 1925, was the first ethnological monograph. His later works on folk beliefs and traditions appeared in English.— Bálint Sándor's work was devoted primarily to customs of religious origin. Margit Luby described the social customs and superstitious rituals of Szamoshát and Nyírség, two regions of Hungary.—Károly Marót wrote some important theoretical essays on ritual poetry.

Several new and significant theoretical ideas and methods of work were introduced in the years prior to the Second World War. Gyula Ortutay and later Linda Dégh, József Faragó, András Benedek and Lajos Vargyas worked **78** out a new scientific approach in the collection of dramatic customs in Hungary. Ortutay's methods of collecting material appeared in the 1956 volume of *Ethnographia (Kérdőív betlehemes játékok gyűjtéséhez* [Questionnaire on the Collection of Nativity Plays]).

Gyula László and László K. Kovács introduced a complex, analytical method in which archaeological and ethnographical findings were both taken into consideration.

The study of folk customs continued with renewed vigour after the Second World War. János Manga, whose first collection of folk customs appeared before the First World War, carried on with his research into Hungarian seasonal festivals. *(Ünnepi szokások a Nyitra megyei Menyhén* [Festive Customs in the Village of Menyhe (Mechenice), Nyitra County], 1942; *Ünnepek, szokások az Ipoly mentén* [Festivals and Customs by the River Ipoly], 1968.)

Hungarian folklorists have written voluminous works on the songs, dialogues and games accompanied by singing that are connected with folk traditions. (*A Magyar Népzene Tára; Corpus Musicae Popularis Hungaricae* edited by Béla Bartók and Zoltán Kodály: Vol. I, György Kerényi: *Gyermekjátékok* [Children's Games]; Vol. II, György Kerényi: *Jeles napok* [Calendar Customs Songs]; Vol. III/A–III/B, Lajos Kiss: *Lakodalom* [Wedding Songs]; Vol. IV, György Kerényi: *Párosítók* [Pairing Songs]; Vol. V, Lajos Kiss and Benjámin Rajeczky: *Siratók* [Laments].)

Specialists in popular beliefs, like Vilmos Diószegi and Éva Cs. Pócs, following the example of Ipolyi, studied the elements of popular beliefs in Hungarian customs.

Research on the historical development of dramatic traditions was begun by Ferenc Hont and continued by Tibor Kardos and Tekla Dömötör.

The interest shown in the social function of folk customs has also increased. In addition to the work of Lajos Kiss, which is now considered a classic, Edit Fél, Judit Morvay, Tamás Hofer, Erzsébet F. Györgyi and Imre Németh have also carried out investigations from a new social angle. Tibor Bodrogi threw light on the theoretical questions of social anthropology.

Popular beliefs, folk-acting and social analysis are studied together in the works of Zoltán Újváry and Imre Ferenczi.

Information on the customs and culture of the Hungarian people at the time of the Conquest of Hungary can be found in the archaeological and **79** historical works of Antal Bartha, István Dienes, Gyula László, Béla Szőke and György Györffy, among others.

Károly Tagányi was the first to collect and study the legal customs of Hungary *(A hazai élő jogszokások gyűjtéséről* [An Anthology of Living Legal Customs in Hungary], 1919). His work has been carried on by László Papp, Ernő Tárkány Szücs and others.

Most authors mentioned also aimed at comparing Hungarian customs with those of the surrounding peoples. Special essays deal with the folk customs of ethnic minorities living in Hungary.

BIBLIOGRAPHY

Iván Balassa: "A magyar temetők néprajzi kutatása" [Ethnographical Research into Hungarian Cemeteries]. *Ethnographia* 84 (1973), 225–242. **81**

Sándor Bálint: *Népünk ünnepei* [The Festivities of Our People]. Budapest, 1938.

Antal Bartha: *A IX–X. századi magyar társadalom* [Hungarian Society in the Ninth and Tenth Centuries]. Budapest, 1968.

András Benedek: "Les jeux hongrois de Noël". *Folia Ethnographica*, 1950, 55–94.

Tibor Bodrogi: *Társadalmak születése* [The Birth of Societies]. Budapest, 1962.

Éva Cs. Pócs: "Zagyvarékas néphite" [Popular Beliefs in Zagyvarékas]. *Néprajzi Közlemények* 10 (1965).

István Dienes: *The Hungarians Cross the Carpathian Basin*. Budapest, 1972.

István Dienes: "Honfoglalóink halottas szokásainak egyik ugor kori eleméről" [Ugrian Elements in the Burial Customs of the Hungarian People at the Time of the Conquest]. *Archaeologiai Értesítő*, 1963.

Vilmos Diószegi: *A sámánhit emlékei a magyar népi műveltségben* [The Remains of Shamanism in Hungarian Folk Culture]. Budapest, 1958.

Tekla Dömötör: "Erscheinungsformen des Charivari im ungarischen Sprachgebiet". *Acta Ethnographica* VI (1957), 73–89.

Tekla Dömötör: *Naptári ünnepek—népi színjátszás* [Seasonal Festivals—Folk Plays]. Budapest, 1964.

Tekla Dömötör: "Ungarischer Volksglauben und Ungarische Volksbräuche zwischen Ost und West". In: *Europa et Hungaria*. Budapest, 1965. 311–322.

Tekla Dömötör: "Das Blochziehen in Rábatótfalu". In: *Kontakte und Grenzen*. Göttingen, 1968.

Tekla Dömötör: "Masken in Ungarn". In: *Masken und Maskenbrauchtum aus Ost- und Südosteuropa*. Basel, 1968.

Tekla Dömötör: "Mythical Elements in Hungarian Midwinter Quête Songs". *Acta Ethnographica* 19 (1970), 119–146.

Tekla Dömötör: *A népszokások költészete* (Folk Poetry Connected with Customs). Budapest, 1974

Edit Fél–Tamás Hofer: *Proper Peasants.* Budapest, 1969. Viking Fund Publications.

Imre Ferenczi–Zoltán Újváry: "Farsangi dramatikus játékok Szatmárban" [Folk Plays at Carnival Time in Szatmár]. *Műveltség és Hagyomány* 4 (1962).

György Györffy: *Tanulmányok a magyar állam eredetéről* [Studies on the Origin of the Hungarian State]. Budapest, 1958.

György Györffy (ed.): *A magyarok elődeiről és a honfoglalásról* [Hungarian Ancestors and Conquest]. Budapest, 1958.

Erzsébet Györgyi: "A tojáshímzés díszítménykincse" [Der Ornamentschatz der verzierten Eier]. *Néprajzi Értesítő* 61 (1974), 5–86.

Tamás Hoffmann: *Néprajz és feudalizmus* [Ethnography and Feudalism]. Budapest, 1975.

István Imreh: *A rendtartó székely falu* [The Székely Village]. Orderly Bucureşti, 1973.

Arnold Ipolyi: *Magyar mythologia* [Hungarian Mythology]. Budapest, 1929 (third edition).

Tibor Kardos–Tekla Dömötör: *Régi magyar drámai emlékek* [Old Hungarian Dramas], Vols. I–II. Budapest, 1960.

Lajos Katona: *Folklore-Kalendárium* [Folklore Calendar]. Budapest, 1912.

György Kerényi: "Jeles napok" [Calendar Customs Songs]. Budapest, 1953. *Corpus Musicae Popularis Hungaricae II.*

Lajos Kiss: *A szegény emberek élete* [The Life of Poor People]. Budapest, 1955.

Lajos Kiss: "Lakodalom" [Wedding Songs]. Budapest, 1955–1956. *Corpus Musicae Popularis Hungaricae III/A–III/B.*

Lajos Kiss–Benjámin Rajeczky: "Siratók" [Laments]. Budapest, 1966. *Corpus Musicae Popularis Hungaricae V.*

László K. Kovács: *A kolozsvári hóstátiak temetkezése* [The Burial Rites in Kolozsvár]. Kolozsvár, 1944.

Gyula László: *A honfoglaló magyar nép élete* [Life of the Hungarian People at the Time of the Conquest]. Budapest, 1944.

Margit Luby: *A parasztélet rendje* [The Order of Peasant Life]. Budapest, 1935.

László Mándoki: *Busójárás Mohácson* ["Busó" Carnival in Mohács]. Pécs, 1973.

János Manga: *Ünnepi szokások a Nyitra megyei Menyhén* [Festive Customs in the Village of Menyhe (Mechenice), Nyitra County]. Budapest, 1942.

János Manga: *Ünnepek, szokások az Ipoly mentén* [Festivals and Customs by the River Ipoly]. Budapest, 1968.

János Manga: "A magyarországi 'kiszehajtás' történeti rétegei" [The Historical Elements of the Custom of Throwing a Straw Dummy in Hungary]. *MTA I. Oszt. Közl.* 26 (1970), 113–142.

János Manga: "Varianten der Hochzeitslieder eines Dorfes". *Acta Ethnographica* 19 (1970), 247–279.

Károly Marót: "Szent Iván napja" [Saint John's Day]. *Ethnographia* 50 (1939), 254–296.

Judit Morvay: *Asszonyok a nagycsaládban* [The Women in the Extended Family]. Budapest, 1956.

Dezső Nagy: "A magyar fejfák és díszítményeik" [Hungarian Wooden Grave Posts]. *Folklór Archívum* 2 (1974).

Gyula Ortutay: "Kérdőív betlehemes játékok gyűjtéséhez" [Questionnaire on the Collection of Nativity Plays]. *Ethnographia* 67 (1956), 91–98.

Gyula Ortutay: *Kleine ungarische Volkskunde*. Budapest, 1963.

László Papp: *Kiskunhalas népi jogélete* [Popular Law in Kiskunhalas]. Budapest, 1941.

Sándor Réső Ensel: *Magyarországi népszokások* [Folk Customs in Hungary]. Pest, 1867.

Géza Róheim: "Hungarian Calendar Customs". *Journal of the Royal Anthropological Institute* (1926), 361–384.

Gyula Sebestyén: *Regös énekek* [Wassailing Songs]. Budapest, 1902. "Magyar Népköltési Gyűjtemény" [Anthology of Hungarian Folk Poetry] 4.

Gyula Sebestyén: *A regösök* [The Wassailers]. Budapest, 1902. "Magyar Népköltési Gyűjtemény" 5.

Zsigmond Szendrey–Ákos Szendrey: "Szokások" [Customs]. *A Magyarság Néprajza* [Hungarian Ethnography], Vol. IV. Budapest, 1937.

Béla Szőke: *A honfoglaló és kora Árpád-kori magyarság régészeti emlékei* [Hungarian Archaeological Relics from the Time of the Conquest and Early Árpádian Era]. Budapest, 1962.

Károly Tagányi: *A hazai élő jogszokások gyűjtéséről* [An Anthology of Living Legal Customs in Hungary]. Budapest, 1919.

Ernő Tárkány Szücs: *Vásárhelyi testamentumok* [Testaments from Vásárhely]. Budapest, 1961.

Zoltán Újváry: "Az agrárkultusz kutatása a magyar és az európai folklórban" [Research into the Agrarian Cults in Hungarian and European Folklore]. *Műveltség és Hagyomány* 11 (1969).

Zoltán Újváry: "Das Begräbnis parodierende Spiele in der ungarischen Volksüberlieferung". *Österreichische Zeitschrift für Volkskunde.* N.S. 20, 1966, 267–276.

Károly Viski: *Hungarian Peasant Customs.* Budapest, 1932.

Henrik Wlislocki: *Aus dem Volksleben der Magyaren.* München, 1893.

LIST OF BLACK-AND-WHITE PLATES

LIST OF COLOUR PLATES

2 *Mummery on St. Lucy's Day. Horvátkimle, Győr-Sopron County, 1969.*

◄ *1 St. Lucy's Day. Újkér, Győr-Sopron County, 1969.*

3 *St. Lucy's coming! Horvátkimle, Győr-Sopron County, 1969.* ►

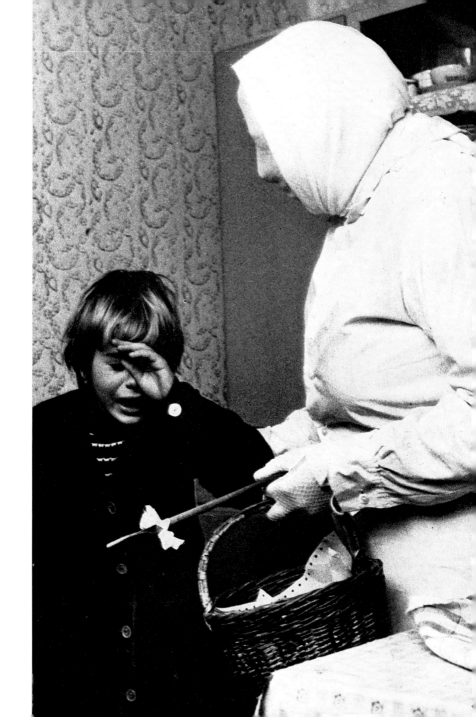

4 Masquerading on December 6th. Horvátkimle, Győr-Sopron County, 1969.

5 Masquerading on December 6th. Horvátkimle, Győr-Sopron County, 1969.

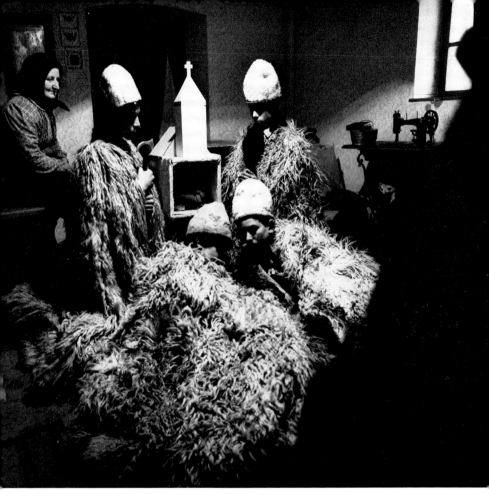

6 *The Nativity players. Szakmár, Bács-Kiskun County, 1969.*

7 *The Nativity play in progress. Szakmár, Bács-Kiskun County, 1969.* ▶

8 *Nativity play presented by Székelys resettled from Bucovina. Kakasd, Tolna County, 1971.*

9 Masked shepherd in a Nativity play. Kéty, Tolna County, 1971.

10 The firemen of Vörs carrying the puppet theatre. Vörs, Somogy County, 1971.

11 "Hej, regö rejtem". Wassailing boys in Újkér, Győr-Sopron County, 1969. ▶

12 The Three Magi. Szakmár, Bács-Kiskun County, 1970.

13 The Three Magi and the star. Szakmár, Bács-Kiskun County, 1970. ▶

15 *"Busó" carnival in Mohács, Baranya County, 1970.*

16 *The boys are not allowed to wear the wooden masks yet. Mohács, Baranya County, 1970.* ▶

◀ 14 *"Busó" carnival in Mohács, Baranya County, 1970.*

18 Masqueraders at Carnival time "scaring" the passengers of a train. Moha, Fejér County, 1970.

◀ 17 "Busó" masqueraders round the fire. Mohács, Baranya County, 1970.

19 A masquer on Shrove Tuesday up to some dirty tricks. Moha, Fejér County, 1970. ▶

20 The pulling of the log in Rábatótfalu, Vas County, 1968. ▶

21 The straw dummy. Kartal, Pest County, 1970. ▶ ▶

23 Painted eggs for the sprinklers. Kazár, Nógrád County, 1970.

◀ *22 Easter sprinkling. Acsa, Pest County, 1971.*

25 Celebrating the grape harvest. Mátramindszent, Nógrád Connty, 1969.

◀ *24 Whitsun Queen. Vitnyéd, Győr-Sopron County, 1970.*

26 Celebrating the grape harvest. Olaszliszka, Borsod-Abaúj-Zemplén County, 1971.

27 Dressing the bride. Kazár, Nógrád County, 1970. ▶

◄ *28 A bride in Sárköz. Decs, Tolna County, 1970.*

29 Wedding procession with flags. Szebény, Baranya County, 1971.

5.12